D1287653

perspectives
ON DESIGN
GREAT LAKES

729 P

Published by

PANACHE
PANACHE PARTNERS

Panache Partners, LLC
1424 Gables Court
Plano, TX 75075
469.246.6060
Fax: 469.246.6062
www.panache.com

Publishers: Brian G. Carabet and John A. Shand

Copyright © 2010 by Panache Partners, LLC
All rights reserved.

No part of this book may be reproduced or transmitted in any form or by any means, electronic or mechanical, including photocopying, recording or by any information storage or retrieval system, except brief excerpts for the purpose of review, without written permission of the publisher.

All images in this book have been reproduced with the knowledge and prior consent of the professionals concerned and no responsibility is accepted by the producer, publisher, or printer for any infringement of copyright or otherwise arising from the contents of this publication. Every effort has been made to ensure that credits accurately comply with the information supplied.

Printed in Malaysia

Distributed by Independent Publishers Group
800.888.4741

PUBLISHER'S DATA

Perspectives on Design Great Lakes

Library of Congress Control Number: 2010924111

ISBN 13: 978-1-933415-80-2
ISBN 10: 1-933415-80-0

First Printing 2010

10 9 8 7 6 5 4 3 2 1

Right: Deep River Partners, page 37

Previous Page: Angelini & Associates Architects, page 25

This publication is intended to showcase the work of extremely talented people. The publisher does not require, warrant, endorse, or verify any professional accreditations, educational backgrounds, or professional affiliations of the individuals or firms included herein. All copy and photography published herein has been reviewed and approved as free of any usage fees or rights and accurate by the individuals and/or firms included herein.

Panache Partners, LLC, is dedicated to the restoration and conservation of the environment. Our books are manufactured with strict adherence to an environmental management system in accordance with ISO 14001 standards, including the use of paper from mills certified to derive their products from well-managed forests. We are committed to continued investigation of alternative paper products and environmentally responsible manufacturing processes to ensure the preservation of our fragile planet.

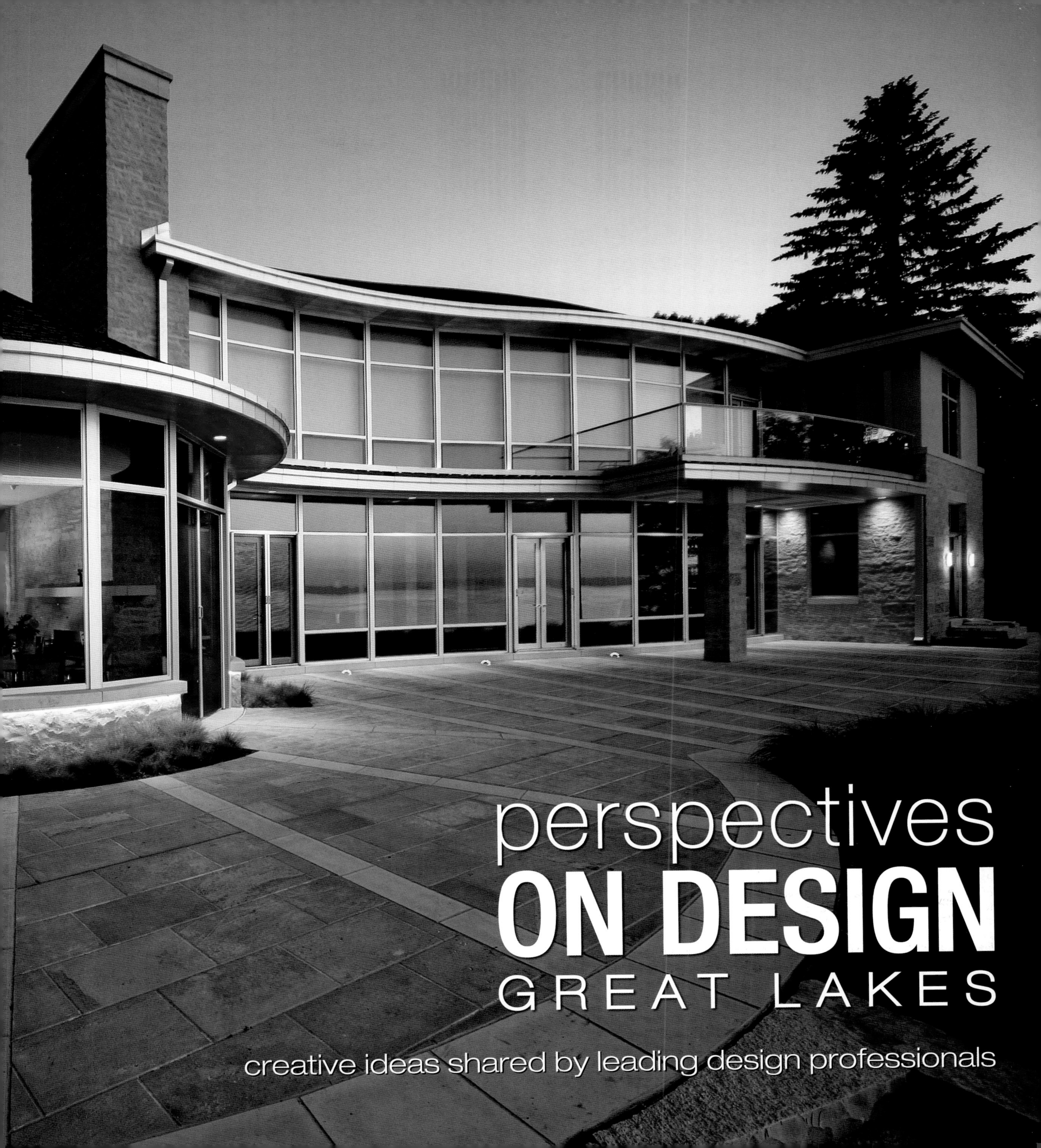

perspectives ON DESIGN GREAT LAKES

creative ideas shared by leading design professionals

DesRosiers Architects, page 49

introduction

Glass Tek, page 161

Vogue Furniture, page 199

Creating the spaces in which we live and achieving the beauty we desire can be a daunting quest—a quest that is as diverse as each of our unique personalities. For some, it may be a serene outdoor living area; for others it may be an opulent marble entryway. Aspiring chefs may find a kitchen boasting the finest in technology their true sanctuary.

Perspectives on Design Great Lakes is a pictorial journey from conceptualizing your dream home to putting together the finishing touches to creating an outdoor oasis. Alongside the phenomenal photography, you will have a rare insight to how these tastemakers achieve such works of art and be inspired by their personal perspectives on design.

Within these pages, the region's finest artisans will share their wisdom, experience, and talent. It is the collaboration between these visionaries and the outstanding pride and craftsmanship of the products showcased that together achieve the remarkable. Learn from leaders in the industry about the aesthetics of finely crafted furnishings, how appropriate lighting can dramatically change the appearance of a room, and what is necessary to create exquisite custom millwork and rugs.

Whether your dream is to have a new home or one that has been redesigned to suit your lifestyle, *Perspectives on Design Great Lakes* will be both an enjoyable journey and a source of motivation.

Arcways, page 137

contents

concept + structure

elements of structure

elements of design

living the elements

Hammond Beeby Rupert Ainge, page 61

Bosco Building Company, Inc., page 99

Jean Stoffer Design, page 177

MOD Interiors, page 153

"The beauty of great design is apparent in every detail."

—Cheryl Nestro

Allegretti Architects, page 13

Tutto Interiors, page 165

Allegretti Architects, page 13

Angelini & Associates Architects, page 25

concept

Deep River Partners, page 37

DesRosiers Architects, page 49

Hammond Beeby Rupert Ainge, page 61

Architecture was instilled in John Allegretti, FAIA, during his childhood. At the age of nine, he helped his father, an architect, build a home in the Lake Michigan sand dunes. The project became a laboratory learning experience and inspired in John the love of craft and construction design as well as landscaping. He continued through high school and earned a degree in architecture at the University of Arkansas with further studies at the University of Illinois.

Travel has played a big role in John's development as one of southeast Michigan's foremost architects. He realized his love for blending nature and human space and responds by articulating design to blend nature into the home, such as an entry that progresses from space to space and utilizes views, trees, and water elements to marry a structure harmoniously with its environment.

Over the past 20 years, Allegretti has entrusted many of his custom homes to Construction Service Associates. Owner Keith McLean and superintendent Kevin Shurbet have a passion for custom homes executed with design integrity. Their work rigorously adds the ingredients necessary to help create the memorably sculptural details that set these homes apart.

"Volume makes a space more interesting. You want to really celebrate that sense of movement and being alive, then capitalize on the views and the way the room works."

—John Allegretti

Allegretti Architects

ABOVE: Set amongst mature, breathtaking trees, the whole house becomes alive in the afternoon. Open area views from the upper level beneath the outwardly projected roofline allow for relaxing times with nature. We worked with Construction Service Associates to actualize the modern home.

FACING PAGE: During sunset, marvelous wave patterns reflect onto the family room ceiling on the bottom deck level. We used bluestone and patches of drywall for the fireplace. The heavy Douglas fir beams create a rigid form within the structure.

PREVIOUS PAGES LEFT: The trellis and glass façade hide the door and blend nicely with the mysterious elements of nature. With a wraparound porch and all-glass railing, the house offers panoramic views of Magician Lake.

PREVIOUS PAGES RIGHT: The sunny south orientation brightens the entry side of the house. Trellis work in the landscaping extends the interior of the house outside, making the area more of a courtyard space. The changing shadows throughout the day create a human scale element with the stained trellis, developing like a sundial as the day progresses. Glue-laminated Douglas fir overhang beams contrast the stainless-steel roof.

Photographs by Jim Yochum

"Great designs emulate the boundless mysteries of nature."

—John Allegretti

ABOVE: Conforming to environmental rules, we worked throughout the project with Construction Service Associates, initially raising the house to accommodate a tall sand dune in front. Inside, the house continues to rise with a pronounced stair tower leading to the upper balcony with skylights and Douglas fir ceiling overlooking the entry. Adorned with glass railings, a cedar bridge from the main floor extends out over the sand dune and attaches to a walkway and stairs that curve and flow to the form of the dunes down to the shore of Lake Michigan.
Left photograph by Jeff Garland
Right photographs by Jim Yochum

FACING PAGE: Adding a second floor, octagon room, and detached garage, we renovated and substantially transformed the entire house, which was built in the early '70s. The kitchen, living room, and dining rooms are on the main floor, and the observation area on the second floor next to the chimneys allows the family to watch their creek flow to Lake Michigan.
Photographs by Jim Yochum

"The lines of the home are meant to develop a sense of order and organization in the horizontal plane."

—John Allegretti

ABOVE & FACING PAGE: The home needed a lot of work, so we worked with Construction Service Associates to take it down to the studs and build the structure anew. We built a new roof, extending it out to create a screened porch on the second floor. The new cement board siding and cedar decking and trellis gives the exterior a multicolor effect while maintaining the footprint and ridgeline. Adding a dormer on posts over the entry made room for a new bedroom, and it also shelters the entry, creating a porch below. The south face collects dappled light, a very Arts-and-Crafts response to a family's second home.
Photographs by John Allegretti

"A creative response melds words into pictures, creating a three-dimensional space."

—John Allegretti

ABOVE: For outdoor entertaining, the pool house features a bar and outside kitchen set. A walkway bridges the passage from the bluff to the swimming pool. The vertical entryway element continues as an interior promenade that extends through the house. The barrel-vaulted segment on the left contains the bedroom space, including a master bedroom sitting area that affords spectacular views of the lake.

FACING PAGE: The residents liked curves and wanted a nautical feel within the space, so we designed the home like a boat. The tall windows face the lake and allow light through the entry, giving the space an open feeling, like being under a beach umbrella. Dark mahogany wood floors with maple accent and brass inlay contrast the ceiling, which bounces light back down.
Photographs by Jim Yochum

"A home that complements the surrounding environment allows its residents and their guests to commune with nature."

—John Allegretti

ABOVE & RIGHT: For a lakeside home, we used sunflower yellow vertical aluminum siding with fiberglass overhangs that act as a trellis, allowing light to filter through the windows while protecting the glass. The family room and guest bedrooms are on the lower level, the living area in the middle, bedrooms above that, and a loft area at the top of the house for viewing the lake.

FACING PAGE: We took a very green approach to the cozy modern home by specifying bamboo flooring and milk paint, a sustainable antiquing finish. The tinted sloping glass walls grade darker toward the top, cutting out UV rays while allowing natural light into the home's public area. A steel truss supports the entire roof for that section, and for the floor, we used Devonian bluestone quarried in New York.
Photographs by Jim Yochum

Bradford and Theresa Angelini seek to create timeless beauty, and when designing a home, each decision they make moves toward achieving that goal. With nearly identical formal educations, the couple's roots are firmly planted in a traditional architecture based on the integrity of materials. Their common ground enables the pair to efficiently collaborate and develop forward-thinking architectural solutions that reflect their backgrounds and values. In 1989, Angelini & Associates Architects began with its two founding members and has grown over the years to include some of the region's most talented designers and architects. The partners embrace an artful design approach with an emphasis on strong, innovative problem-solving. The team considers a variety of alternatives for every challenge, knowing that allowing a creative design process brings about the best results. Remaining uncommitted to a single architectural style, the firm creates structures that reflect design integrity—holding true to the purpose of the individual project. Each house is a culmination of materials, ideas, and decisions based on collaboration with the owner's needs and desires, interpreted into built form.

"Working in an area that sets high intellectual and artistic expectations means constant stimulation and ever-changing challenges."

—Theresa Angelini

ANGELINI & ASSOCIATES ARCHITECTS

"Good aesthetics requires a patient search."

—Bradford Angelini

ABOVE: With an elevated floor and a low ceiling, the intimate dining room at Windy Crest opens to the sky above by extending the glass wall horizontally onto the ceiling plane. The panoramic southern views of the city below allowed for solar gain that we controlled by detailing concealed motorized shades within the structure of the roof and buffet cabinetry below the window.
Photograph by Jason B. Wise

FACING PAGE: The house on Heatherway is composed of three primary building blocks organized around an open courtyard to allow for natural light and protected views to the adjacent rooms. The linear circulation axis links the front entry hall, formal dining room, and great room, with the adjacent courtyard overlapping the interior spaces. The main stair incorporates metal framing, thin maple treads, open risers, and natural lighting from the skylight above to create an airy yet sculptural centerpiece. In collaboration with Sally Klein Interiors, we achieved the perfect finishes.
Photographs by Jeff Garland Photography

PREVIOUS PAGES LEFT: The homeowner wanted a sleek, efficient kitchen without sacrificing comfort or function. We used contemporary clean materials and minimalist details combined with an open floorplan to achieve this goal. Cabinets, appliances, and lighting reinforce the home's interior and exterior aesthetic. Lowering the ceiling plane defines the space as more intimate within the larger volume of the great room and casual dining area.
Photograph by Jeff Garland Photography

PREVIOUS PAGES RIGHT: Exterior elements of the Heatherway home harmonize for a crisp look: cool grey roof shingles, smooth dark purple brick, and clear vertical cedar paneled siding with a pickled stain. The second-floor massing appears to float above the structure below, emphasized by the cantilever and the high, horizontal window bands.
Photograph by Jeff Garland Photography

"Every challenge deserves the consideration of three to five solutions; the best one will certainly win out."

—Bradford Angelini

RIGHT: The winged roof angles crown the hilltop house and give it a commanding presence. We used an inverted-pitched roof within the exercise room to allow for tall windows and a high ceiling within, focusing views to the outdoors. Working with Terrafirma, Inc. on landscaping and construction, we created an unforgettable home. Exterior deck platforms below compose a dynamic path through a pond and stream, offering a geometrically constructed base to the house within the larger natural setting.
Photograph by Gary Easter Photographics

"The more engaged the homeowner, the better the home."

—Theresa Angelini

ABOVE: The home at Heron Oaks sits gently within a wooded area, with an entry sequence that captures the tranquility of both the natural surroundings and the home's interior. Upon approaching the entry, the butterfly roof of the informal dining space and the gabled guest wing frame the front porch. The Mondrian-inspired pattern of the siding provides subtle, clean geometric lines for added visual interest.

FACING PAGE: The interior spaces adjacent to the enclosed courtyard appear to extend into the outdoor space. We reinforced this by the use of floor tile on both the floor surface of the interior spaces and the perimeter ground plane of the exterior. White stucco walls reflect light into the adjacent hall, entry, and great room. At the screened porch, the Mondrian influence appears in the screen divisions, providing a foreground to the views beyond.
Photographs by Jeff Garland Photography

"Tried-and-true materials offer an advantage; they create handsome, naturally sustainable, and durable architecture."

—Theresa Angelini

ABOVE: Timber-framed mountain homes served as the inspiration for this timeless house on the ravine at Delhi Glen; we worked with Christian Tennant Custom Homes on development and construction. Window openings, stone, natural cedar, board and batten siding, and exposed timber are composed in horizontal and vertical patterns that create a balanced complexity of color and texture with a sense of scale.
Photograph by Bradford Angelini

RIGHT: We knew that finding the correct proportions and spacing for the exposed trusses was crucial—it was important to give scale to the room without overwhelming the space. Visually light, the custom hand-hewn trusses contrast with the massive stone fireplace to add interest and a human dimension to the room. With the help of Nicolette Bozsik Interiors, we created an overall look that offers elegance with a warm, rustic quality.
Photograph by Beth Singer

FACING PAGE: Thanks to collaboration with Donna Newsom Interiors and builder Christopher J.R. Laycock, the dining and living spaces at Cobblestone Farm employ a traditional architectural vocabulary—while still meeting exacting LEED technical construction standards. The exterior shell of insulated concrete forms is clad in wood siding, cultured stone, and drywall, creating warm, comfortable spaces on the interior. Windows and doors are proportioned to a residential scale and natural daylight highlights the radiant heated tile floors and pickled wood walls and ceiling.
Photographs by Jeff Garland Photography

"Something as simple as using three-dimensional models will engage others to give constructive design criticism, improving the outcome."

—Bradford Angelini

LEFT: The owner of the house on Indian River has a passionate interest in Tibetan art and architecture, which we reflected in the design of a tapered meditation tower inspired by those forms. We used clean lines of the stucco tower as a contrast to the textured horizontal cedar siding on the body of the house. Inside, the simplicity of the stair makes a striking impression. Natural light from the meditation space at the top of the tower filters through the stair treads to the level below.

FACING PAGE: Working closely with builder Paul Dannels, we translated the owner's desire to have a study with pilot-seat views into a symbolic tree house nestled between the main house and the meditation tower. A Y-shaped timber structure represents the trunk and branches while a cantilevered porch creates a platform. The roof serves as the tree canopy, with open framing filtering the sunlight, creating patterns on the wall of the home.
Photographs by Jeff Garland Photography

With more than 30 years of experience in residential architecture, design principal Richard Sherer and his sister, interior designer Susan Sherer, joined forces in 1999 to establish Deep River Partners. Descendents of painters and sculptors, their father and uncle were nationally known Milwaukee-based architects. Richard and Susan grew up on the shores of Lake Michigan, building snow forts, tree houses, and sandcastles—the beginning of the creative legacy their father passed along to them. As the two matured in their family of 11, they developed their design acumen and an acute understanding of "home."

Providing a holistic approach to residential design, the firm combines the disciplines of architecture, interior design, lighting design, and landscape design into a seamless whole. Deep River Partners leads a team of artisans, craftsmen, and consultants who bring the design vision into reality. The team maintains the highest standards of quality as they translate client goals into layered environments that are rich in detail, evoking an emotional response. Through assessment and definition of people, place, and purpose, they use their inspiration to forge award-winning designs that encourage their residents to flourish.

"Our team utilizes the gifts of creativity, insight, introspection, and experience—the result is residential design that consistently engages the heart, mind, and soul."

—Richard Sherer

Deep River Partners

"The thoughtful composition of many parts is the essence of timeless design."

—Susan Sherer

ABOVE: Providing movement and strength, marching Lannon stone columns blur the line between inside and outside and further highlight the lake beyond. Natural materials and warm colors provide golden light. Topped with a cherry handrail, the metalwork is a continuous ribbon, a stylized natural pattern that appears unsupported as the railing ascends to the second floor.
Photograph by Joe De Maio

FACING PAGE TOP: Like spokes coming out of a hub, subtle ribs in the drywall create a radiating ceiling relief that pierces the curve of the outside wall. Designed by nationally recognized lighting consultant Steven L. Klein, IALD, LC, of Klein Lighting, Milwaukee, Wisconsin, architecturally integrated and special-effect lighting enhances the purity of the natural materials in slight tension with the clean architectural forms. Uplighting from the floor illuminates the aluminum glass wall mullions, enhancing their flowing rhythm.
Photograph by Mark Heffron

FACING PAGE BOTTOM LEFT: Emulating the concept of a jewelry box, the exterior walls of the dining room are clad with 2-by-2-foot cherry panels with rotating grain. Subtle and simply refined appointments warm and soften the interior. The shimmering silk wall-covering echoes tall beach grasses catching the sun.
Photograph by Mark Heffron

FACING PAGE BOTTOM RIGHT: Warm cherry casework and bamboo floors contrast the cool window frames and stainless-steel appliances. Three soft glass pendants illuminate the cantilevered stone island, and concealed above-cabinet lighting provides an indirect glow of shadowless ambient light.
Photograph by Joe De Maio

PREVIOUS PAGES: Harmonious with the water, the curvilinear wall of floor-to-ceiling glass provides a constant rhythm that stands in partnership with Lake Michigan.
Photograph by Joe De Maio

"The uncluttered atmosphere allows the art collection to speak and command a presence."

—Richard Sherer

ABOVE: Located at the top of Milwaukee's skyline, the condominium offers panoramic views of the Lake Michigan shoreline to the east and the city lights to the west. The opening to the second floor of the unit is punctured by the mirrored shaft. The elliptical rhythm is repeated in the pearlescent balustrade produced by metal artisans Custom Metals of Madison, Wisconsin. Guarded by Rama, fiber optic stars expand the ceiling to infinity.
Photographs by Joe De Maio

FACING PAGE TOP: The library also serves as a media room and overflow space for guests. Walnut panels conceal a large screen television and Murphy bed. Ebony stain highlights the panels, adding accent and contrast. The transitional style is clean without being too contemporary. Uplighting suspends the space between walnut beams and the true ceiling several feet above. The casework displays books and artifacts from the owner's travels.
Photograph by Joe De Maio

FACING PAGE BOTTOM: Anchored by the custom area rug from premier carpet vendor Kashou Carpets, Milwaukee, Wisconsin, the living room is designed in monochromatic tones drawing you outside to the lake and horizon beyond. The rug's circular pattern emulates the cove light above and complements the subtle curves of the furniture. Identified by wall sconces, the repeating cased openings at the room's perimeter frame the panoramic lake views while creating a transition to the contemporary curtainwall beyond.
Photograph by Mark Heffron

"The dance and slight tension between materials create a dynamic environment, one that is alive."

—Richard Sherer

ABOVE: Designed for a family with eight children, honestly expressed natural materials create a durable atmosphere. Exposed steel beams, natural blue stone, and clear maple casework join together to formulate a modern rustic style. Clean lines and hard edges contrast warm materials and the occasional placement of an antique. The natural stone fireplace at the screened porch is the focal point of the vista from the living room.
Photographs by Mark Heffron

FACING PAGE: The roof lines cascade at the sides of the home, nestling it into the shoreline. Landscape architect Peter Kudlata of Flagstone Landscape, Milwaukee, Wisconsin, pulled the home's design themes beyond the exterior walls out toward the lake. The meditation deck with whirlpool, fireplace, and adjoining sitting area opens from the master bedroom. Lifestyle concepts are integrated into the built form, and the geometries break down into the natural setting.
Photographs by Joe De Maio

"A home's beauty is embodied in the subtleties of proportion, scale, rhythm, detail, and fine finishes."

—Richard Sherer

ABOVE LEFT: The lower-level entry takes advantage of the sloping topography. Terraced gardens step up to the screened porch and upper terrace. The thoughtful use of multiple materials—the permanence of stone balanced by plaster, wood panels, and brick accents—supports the home's Old World feel.

ABOVE RIGHT: Cherry paneling defines the fireplace nook and provides concealed log storage behind a secret panel. Bookshelves on the right and a large window seat on the left create the perfect environment to take in the rolling hillside views.

FACING PAGE: The whimsical turret marks the romantic entry into the home. The playful aesthetic is accentuated by such purposeful detailing as varying shaped roof shingles, the copper spire, arched windows, crafted timbers, and brick accenting.

Photographs by Mark Heffron

"The traditional Tudor style is refreshed with an open, airy atmosphere that floods the home with natural light and allows panoramic views."

—Susan Sherer

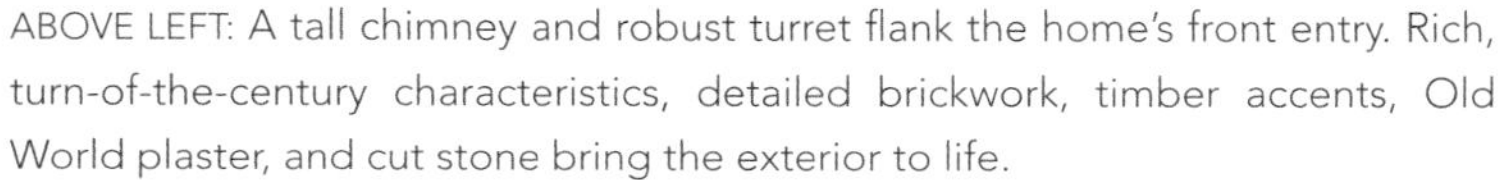

ABOVE LEFT: A tall chimney and robust turret flank the home's front entry. Rich, turn-of-the-century characteristics, detailed brickwork, timber accents, Old World plaster, and cut stone bring the exterior to life.

ABOVE RIGHT: Traditional leaded glass window panes give way to large floor-to-ceiling windows that offer unobstructed views. Accessible from the living and dining rooms, the octagonal sunroom provides a porch atmosphere that can be enjoyed year-round.

FACING PAGE: Accented by wrought-iron balusters, reclaimed newel posts rise in rhythm to the home's second floor. Flanked by a long, curved window seat, the vaulted ceiling and iron chandelier are the central focus of the entry hall. Leaded transoms above the tall windows beckon historical roots while expansive glass brings an abundance of natural light to the interior.
Photographs by Joe De Maio

A third-generation architect, Louis DesRosiers was raised in an atmosphere filled with design and was greatly influenced by his father, Arthur DesRosiers, a renowned Detroit liturgical architect. Because his exposure to the profession began on day one, his talent in design and creativity developed innately. After college in 1976, Louis followed in his father's footsteps and launched his own firm, DesRosiers Architects, from the ground up.

To showcase Michigan's spectacular lakes and topography, the firm integrates glass as one of its primary design elements, resulting in some of the largest expanses in the state. The goal, as Louis points out, is to expand on the views so that they can be appreciated from every space in the house—even the more mundane, such as bathrooms. And to further invite in the breathtaking outdoors of the Great Lakes region, Louis advocates the use of large, screened skylights that open electronically, capturing fresh lake air and natural light.

Aside from capturing the beauty of the outdoors, Louis believes that a structure has to be cozy and warm and that each room offers its own unique enjoyment. First and foremost, his firm designs around the lifestyle and personalities of the homeowners since they are, afterall, the ones who should be rewarded by it every day, not the architects.

"People these days are more informal. When you entertain, everyone ends up in the kitchen—so we decided to move our kitchens into the living areas."

—Louis DesRosiers

DesRosiers Architects

"A good architect will glean information from the homeowners as well as the advantages of the site—such as where the best views are—then creatively forge the data into a design concept."

—Louis DesRosiers

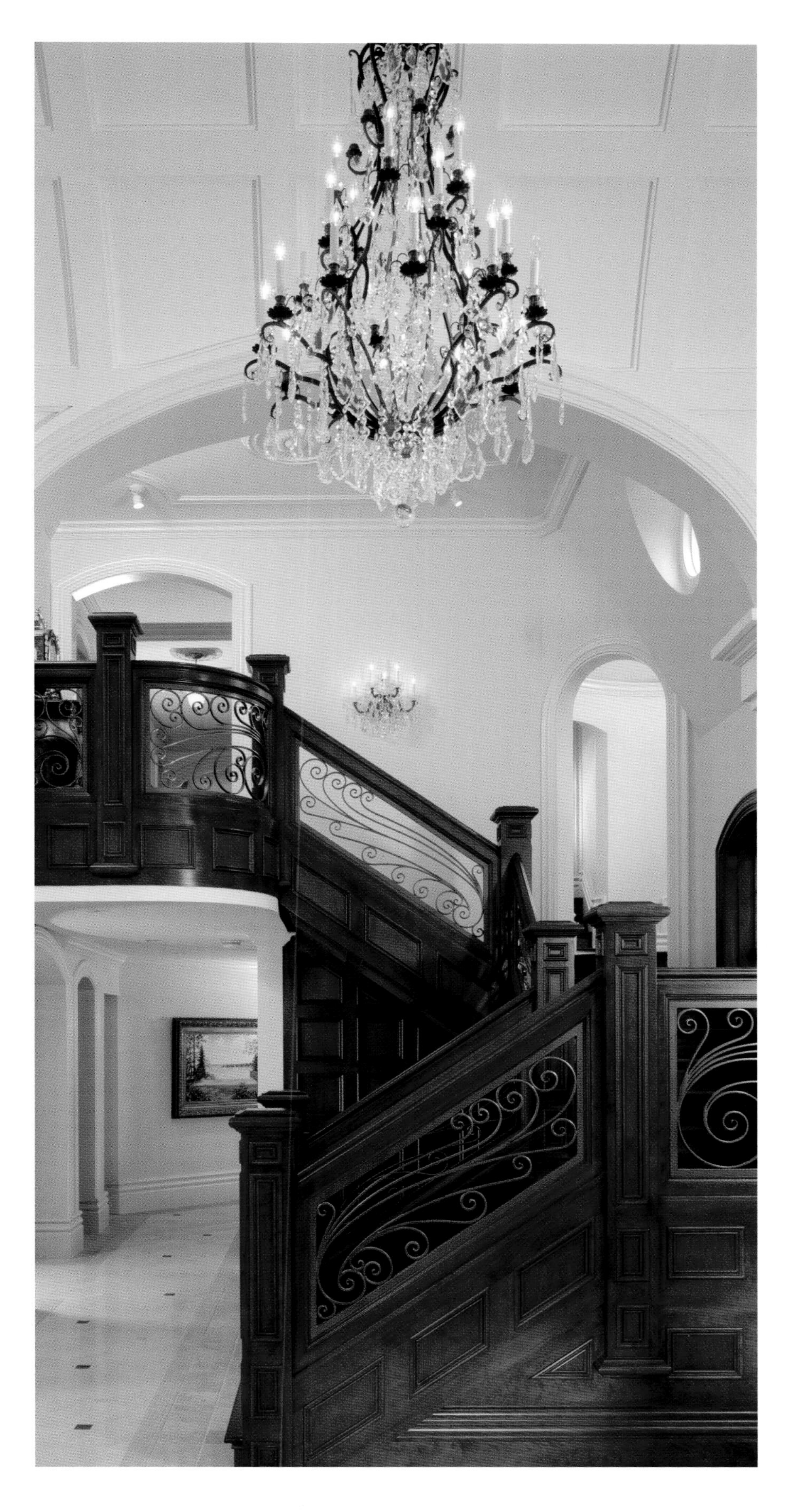

RIGHT: Connecting all three levels of the home, the French chateau-style staircase includes two spacious landings, each turn captured by capped newel posts. The rich, flowing hues of raised cherry wood panels and wrought iron starkly contrast the alabaster surroundings in the foyer arches and the creme marfil marble floor.
Photograph by Beth Singer

FACING PAGE: Old World materials and applications were used to replicate an authentic French chateau, but the technology is nothing short of cutting-edge. Perched on a 35-foot-high bluff overlooking Upper Straits Lake, the majestic home quickly accesses the water's edge with an elevator that travels from the rooftop deck down below the basement to a 90-foot tunnel leading right to the lakeshore.
Photograph by Beth Singer

PREVIOUS PAGES: Inspired by the magnificent panoramic views of Lake Michigan, both houses exemplify a very light and open pavilion concept. In the left image, a fusion of contemporary glass walls with a relaxed cottage style creates a home that brings the outside in. The stone path invites viewers to appreciate the water firsthand. In the right image, formal columns blend with casual furnishings, creating a warm gathering place for friends and family.
Photographs by Glen Rauth

"We are all giant sponges. We absorb the information that we encounter every day in the media and in real life. The artistic challenge is to develop that information into a design concept that satisfies the homeowner's every requirement."

—Louis DesRosiers

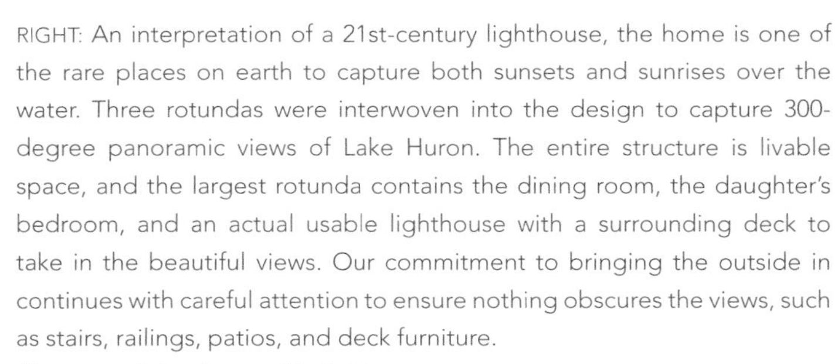

RIGHT: An interpretation of a 21st-century lighthouse, the home is one of the rare places on earth to capture both sunsets and sunrises over the water. Three rotundas were interwoven into the design to capture 300-degree panoramic views of Lake Huron. The entire structure is livable space, and the largest rotunda contains the dining room, the daughter's bedroom, and an actual usable lighthouse with a surrounding deck to take in the beautiful views. Our commitment to bringing the outside in continues with careful attention to ensure nothing obscures the views, such as stairs, railings, patios, and deck furniture.
Photograph by George Dzahristos

"We all draw inspiration and vision from our deepest, innermost levels of creativity."

—Louis DesRosiers

RIGHT: The mahogany entry door opens into a majestic grand foyer with Asian and contemporary architectural components. A floating ceiling allows morning light to enter through clerestory windows, and the ribbon-cut mahogany walls are offset with granite flooring and pillars that continue all the way to the lower level.

FACING PAGE TOP: The home was a unique case undergoing a third renovation after two previous ones by other design firms; its architecture showcases light and shadow. Inside, a newly added foyer transitions from a single story to a very grand two-story space. Wisconsin Fon du Lac pillars trimmed with smooth-faced Indiana limestone brace impressive cantilevers of the cedar shake roof.

FACING PAGE BOTTOM: The stepped, all-copper roof echoes Asian-style architecture while the design stamped into the copper fascia evokes Art Deco. The exterior stone—a combination of smooth-honed and split-face Fon du Lac limestone—elegantly contrasts the driveway pavers, 300-year-old stones recovered from flooded Chinese villages.

Photographs by George Dzahristos

"Human beings inherently like the softness of a curve—it is very pleasant. The contrast of geometric shapes draw the eye because they attract attention and make the space more dynamic."

—Louis DesRosiers

ABOVE: Honed stone walls frame the panoramic lakeview windows of the remarkable great room. A dramatic three-story fireplace of Minnesota's Mankato honed stone with alternating bands of mahogany wood highlights the main floor's soaring spaces. Designed to cast shade and shadow over the fireplace surface, an adjacent skylight enriches every detail.

FACING PAGE: The unique helical staircase serves as a magnificent sculpture in the grand residence's entry. Light from a circular skylight above the foyer bathes the intricately detailed bronze, tempered glass, and mahogany railing. The stair wraps around a 12-foot-diameter opening in the floor, exposing the glow of an illuminated marquee and ticket booth at the lower level's entertainment room.
Photographs by Laszlo Regos

CINEMA

"A soft, monochromatic color palette can balance contrasting materials and transform a space into an atmosphere of quiet, calmness, and serenity."

—Louis DesRosiers

ABOVE: The existing structure was entirely renovated from the room's interior to the exterior glass. The 10-foot-long fireplace features a cantilevered travertine marble mantle and hearth. Locally sourced and ruggedly stacked Fon du Lac stone accentuates the loftiness of the space while contrasting the contemporary room's sharp angles. The left panel of the flowing horizontally grained myrtle wood slides sideways to reveal a 50-inch flatscreen television. Expansive 12-foot glass panes accentuated by live bamboo plants flood the space with light.
Photograph by George Dzahristos

FACING PAGE: This major renovation project began with the construction of an enormous 45-foot-tall rotunda that starts at the home's lowest level and pierces through to a breathtaking dome topped by an eight-foot-diameter skylight. A completely cantilevered library is accessible by an independent tight spiral staircase and floats below the clerestory that lets light in from all directions. With beautifully pilastered columns, creme marfil marble floor, and an attractive curved staircase rising to the second floor, the rotunda is the center of the home, leading to all main rooms.
Photographs by James Haefner

James Wright Hammond founded the firm in Chicago in 1961 on the premise that interaction between client and architect at all stages of the design and construction process produces the best buildings. Today, Thomas Beeby—former Dean of the Yale School of Architecture—and his partners Dennis Rupert and Gary Ainge continue the tradition of a design approach based on collaboration. With a diverse portfolio of work in institutional, educational, liturgical, and residential architecture, the partners have expanded their range nationally beyond the Chicago area.

Neutral in taste, style, and preference, the firm responds to the specific requirements of each project's site and context, which it attempts to reconcile with the individual needs and wants of each client. New designs and details therefore take their surroundings as a primary point of departure; these often extend recognizable architectural styles or blend styles to create a hybrid. Carefully considered details achieve seamless stylistic continuity throughout and emphasize each project as a unique response to a particular set of challenges.

"The serious study of old buildings can lead to an architecture of lasting quality."

—Tom Beeby

Hammond Beeby Rupert Ainge

"Authentic detail and genuine artifacts support each other in a meaningful dialogue."

—Tom Beeby

ABOVE LEFT: Flanked by matching basins and enclosures for the shower and water closet, the bathtub in the master bathroom is surrounded by a mirror-lined canopy, a focal element that adds depth to the room. Onyx is used throughout for the flooring and wainscoting; the cabinetry features custom French millwork.

ABOVE RIGHT & FACING PAGE: Comprising a suite for formal entertaining, the living and dining rooms are arranged along one side of the stair gallery. Windows located at the edges of the dining room reinforce the central placement of the table while in the living room lighting fixtures, furnishings, and hand-carved wall medallions in the style of Louis XV contrast with the restrained classicism of the panel mouldings and door trim. A clear sightline is maintained throughout, and complementary mirrors and chandeliers placed along this line establish the living and dining rooms as a linked pair.

PREVIOUS PAGES LEFT: An oblong gallery with a suspended stair at one end occupies a middle zone between the entrance foyer and the rooms for formal entertaining. The hall's pure geometry and its axially and symmetrically arranged door and window openings exhibit the strict geometry of 18th-century French Neoclassicism, which is softened by the curves of the stair, its balustrade, and the ornamental metalwork of the chandelier and paired wall sconces.

PREVIOUS PAGES RIGHT: On a site full of large coniferous trees, the house's design was inspired by the small chateaux built for members of the French court during the 18th century in the neighborhood of Versailles. Its division into three pavilions separates formal rooms for entertaining from informal living rooms and shapes exterior spaces—like the entry courtyard—as outdoor rooms.
Photographs by John Hall

"Ordinary architectural prose can be elevated to poetry through carefully developed arrangement and finish."

—Tom Beeby

ABOVE: An existing duplex was transformed into a two-story wood-frame house planned throughout according to a four-inch module that left little margin for error, almost like an enlarged work of cabinetry. Precise use of natural materials responded to the site's context and the owner's interest in Asian art. Exposed exterior framing in Douglas fir reveals the major living spaces along one side of the house, with stone fireplaces at each end, and the lateral walls that separate these spaces from a zone of circulation. Large bronze-clad windows and a covered patio space frame spectacular views of the Roaring Fork River.

FACING PAGE: An open kitchen occupies one end of a continuous series of living spaces that run the length of the first floor. Here the emphasis on natural elements found throughout the house—sycamore cabinetwork, wooden floors and ceilings, and moss-stone chimney stacks—is contrasted with stainless-steel appliances and a bronze hearth surround. Interior design firm Leslie Jones & Associates gave the space Asian sensibilities with modern, minimalist furniture.

Photographs by Steve Hall, Hedrich Blessing Photography

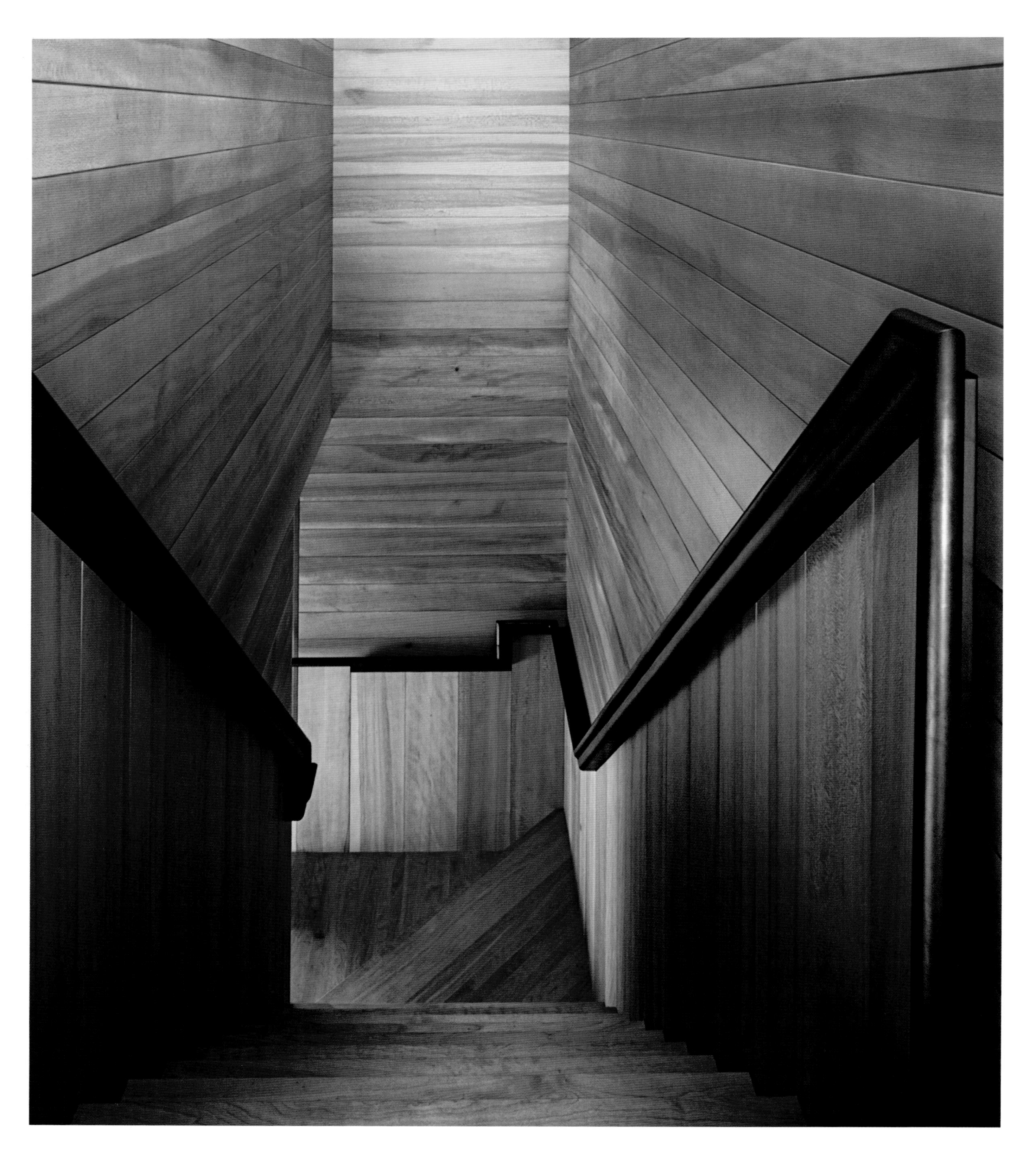

"Material and formal consistency create a home with true repose."

—Tom Beeby

TOP RIGHT: A centrally located library also serves as a light well. Shelf placement and sycamore paneling are dictated by an established four-inch module. The core of the house, the space also opens outward to views of the Roaring Fork River beyond the living room.

BOTTOM RIGHT: In the master bathroom, rich materials are integrated into a uniform surface, with a stainless-steel dado separating an upper zone with sycamore panels and bronze-clad windows from a lower zone of travertine. A flat mirror reinforces the master bathroom's planar qualities.

FACING PAGE: Adopting the four-inch module used throughout the house, the staircase is clad entirely in sycamore paneling, which changes direction to distinguish a wainscot zone beneath the bronze handrail from the wall zone above. Handmade bronze railings conform to the contours of the hand.

Photographs by Steve Hall, Hedrich Blessing Photography

ABOVE: Matching fireplaces in the kitchen and living area bracket a continuous living space faced on one side by bronze-clad windows that stretch from floor to ceiling. These, together with the open-slat decking on the covered patio beyond, dissolve the boundary between inside and outside, a strategy common to both traditional Asian and modern styles of architecture. This continuity with natural surroundings emphasizes this house as a retreat from the city.

FACING PAGE: Set into a native-stone chimney piece, the fireplace surround is forged from a single folded panel of bronze. The adjacent placement of a traditional Asian chair restates a larger theme of rustic simplicity in the company of precise construction.

Photographs by Steve Hall, Hedrich Blessing Photography

Buddhism
FAST AND FLAVORFUL
SPA FOOD
INDIAN ART
INDIAN PAINTING
DICTIONARY
Chinese Celadon Wares
Second City
PHILIP ROTH
Degas
BONNARD
CHICAGO
Encyclopedia of Archaeology
ORIGINS
Henri Rousseau
HERITAGE

"Complementary elements from varying sources can be blended to create an evocative whole."

—Tom Beeby

TOP RIGHT: Reused Southern yellow pine floors run through an open vista along the house's central axis, which is reinforced by a stair landing that makes a covered entry just inside the front door. The fixtures and furniture conform to the Georgian character of the architecture.

BOTTOM RIGHT: Doors are located in the corners of the dining room to hold circulation to its edges, allowing the fireplace and dining table to reinforce the room's central axis. Paneling beneath the windows is pushed slightly forward to emphasize these as freestanding tabernacles. Georgian details and furnishings give the room a simple, formal character.

FACING PAGE: The house combines the formal elements of a mansion—such as the hierarchical arrangement and pure Palladian detailing of this central section—with the domestic character of a New England house, evident in the adjacent clapboard siding and dormer windows. The house's tripartite plan and elegant detailing recall the Hammond-Harwood House in Annapolis, Maryland, designed by William Buckland and constructed in 1774.
Photographs by Judith Bromley

Stanley Tigerman, FAIA, and Margaret McCurry, FAIA, create private residences that vary as much in form and presence as the people for whom they are created, but there is a consistency. The architecture's understated presence exudes simplicity. Precise lines, deft use of materials, and interesting spatial relationships engage all who enter Tigerman-McCurry Architect's innovative structures. It is difficult to articulate their form of genius, but one thing is certain: Stanley and Margaret have been creating veritable works of art for decades.

With projects across the globe, in the world of architecture, people know and respect Stanley and Margaret's work. Stanley received both of his architectural degrees from Yale University and continues to serve on advisory boards at Yale, Princeton, and the Art Institute of Chicago. Margaret earned her art history degree at Vassar and was awarded a Loeb Fellowship for Environmental Design studies at the Graduate School of Design at Harvard. She serves on the boards of both the Textile and Architecture & Design Departments at the Art Institute of Chicago. Working independently, Stanley and Margaret design some of the most expressive dwellings throughout the Great Lakes region, across the country, and internationally, creating a legacy of timeless structures. Their alternative concepts and groundbreaking approaches to designing new ways of living have set a new standard for architects the world over.

"Inspiration comes foremost from the site and the interests of people who will live in the space."

—Margaret McCurry

Tigerman McCurry Architects

"Views to the exterior are an important ingredient in developing the interior space of a dwelling. The architecture should engage all who enter and emphasize the sense of place."

—Margaret McCurry

RIGHT: Recognized by Wisconsin fishermen as a key landmark, the house is pointed like the prow of a ship headed out to sea; lake-facing façades step down concentrically and incrementally to permit maximum lake views. Our V-shaped, butterfly plan allows views up and down the coast from all major family rooms, the master suite, and guest rooms.

PREVIOUS PAGES: Prime waterfront property and the owner's passion for diving led us to create the metaphoric entry design reminiscent of a glowing marine lighthouse. The "Crayola House" front façade seen from a rural gravel road features a transparent glass block entry that is the focal point of the forecourt triangle. Light floods the interior double-height entry, illuminating first-and second-floor halls and stairway. The front door begins an axis that permits direct passage to the kitchen-dining room with views across the cooktop and dining table and on out to the lake. The window above the door is aligned with upper-floor hallway openings to permit views to the woods.

Photographs by Steve Hall, Hedrich Blessing Photography

"Identifiable access, spatial progression, and a sense of openness with centers for interaction are critical to a successful design. As Louis Sullivan averred, a house should possess both function and form."

—Margaret McCurry

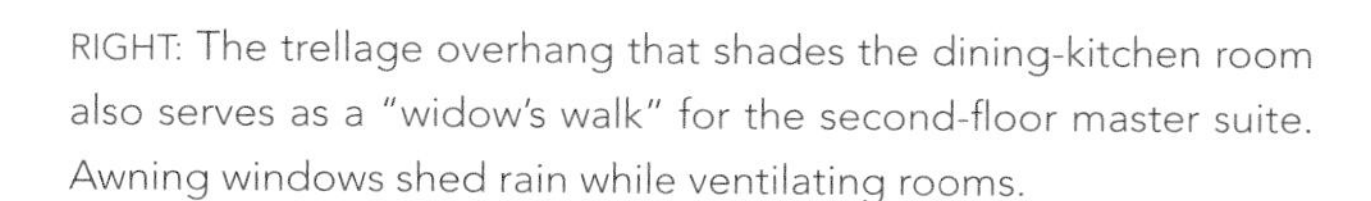

RIGHT: The trellage overhang that shades the dining-kitchen room also serves as a "widow's walk" for the second-floor master suite. Awning windows shed rain while ventilating rooms.

FACING PAGE: The curvilinear double-height entry is the starting point for three axes: one on the right leads to the library-living room; the central axis crosses a circle with a compass inset at its center to the kitchen-dining room with views up and down the beach; the left one beyond the circular staircase leads to the entertainment center. A screened porch offers clear views of the lake, entry court, and woodlands. Corrugated galvanized steel cladding ensures protection from the elements.
Photographs by Steve Hall, Hedrich Blessing Photography

"Designing a house that is light-filled and spatially balanced enhances the quality of life for its residents."

—Margaret McCurry

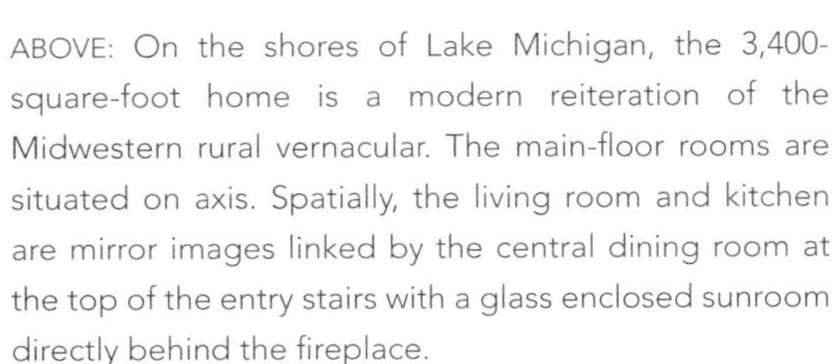

ABOVE: On the shores of Lake Michigan, the 3,400-square-foot home is a modern reiteration of the Midwestern rural vernacular. The main-floor rooms are situated on axis. Spatially, the living room and kitchen are mirror images linked by the central dining room at the top of the entry stairs with a glass enclosed sunroom directly behind the fireplace.

FACING PAGE: "The Blue House" nestled in the dunes is a study in simplicity and symmetry. We designed the house as basically a one-room-deep plan, which permits simultaneous views to the front and rear of the house. The two-and-a-half-story house on the lake elevation has a projecting sunroom with upper deck. A master suite and two children's bedrooms all access the upper deck with guest bedrooms under the eaves; outdoor dining on the patio is directly accessible by kitchen French doors while the adjacent concrete patio is accessed from the living room. Stairs lead down through dune grasses to a sandy beach.

Photographs by Craig Dugan, Hedrich Blessing Photography

"Remote, densely wooded hilly lots can present certain challenges. A house should relate to the topography of the land and take its design cues from that interaction."

—Margaret McCurry

ABOVE: With the central spine of the structure to the left and the kitchen opposite it, the dining room provides gathering space for guests and cooks and maintains its own identity while still remaining part of the great room.

FACING PAGE: The family's "Camp" is sited on the unspoiled sand dunes of Lake Superior in Michigan's Upper Peninsula. Contours of the dunes dictated our stepped plan since building on slopes in excess of 25 percent is forbidden by the Department of Natural Resources. We designed a footprint to fill the flatter land surface in an interesting architectural fashion. A wraparound porch offers a sheltered entry and open sitting area protected from the elements. The exterior features a forest green stained wood façade accented by a practical red asphalt shingled roof pitched to weather the four seasons, especially the heavy snowfalls of the region.
Photographs by Christopher Barrett, Hedrich Blessing Photography

"Bringing the feeling of nature indoors is simply achieved through an open floorplan with abundant windows."

—Margaret McCurry

ABOVE & FACING PAGE: Sited as close to Lake Superior's shore as the DNR would permit, the casual family homestead is meant to endure for future generations to enjoy. We designed the three-story house so the lake is visible from all windows on the north as well as both sides; ceilings are lower in the flanking rooms to create a cozy retreat from the main gathering spaces. All rooms open off of the central family room with its anchoring river rock fireplace for an open, free-flowing aesthetic. Natural timber trusses seem to support high ceilings in this passive solar structure.
Photographs by Christopher Barrett, Hedrich Blessing Photography

Every home starts with a sketch—usually of the floorplan as it relates to the site, sometimes of an exterior elevation. Form follows function, but a good designer can develop both simultaneously. Wayne Visbeen begins with a series of sketches that visually explain the proposed building footprint, interior ceiling volumes, relationship between spaces, and integration of furnishings. His detailed approach ensures that homes are conceptually cohesive, beautiful, and functional.

Wayne and his Visbeen Associates team, which includes associate architects and an interior designer, have designed more than 500 homes and undertaken residential and commercial projects primarily throughout the United States, and also in the Bahamas, Costa Rica, Brazil, the Philippines, China, and several European countries. Their global perspective underscores the importance of designing architecture that is meant for the locale and the individual site. While the firm works in a wide variety of vernaculars, constants include cohesive exterior and interior design, fine finishes, and compositions that unfold organically to reveal something aesthetically engaging around every corner.

"An architect must consider the impact of every element in the design."

—Wayne Visbeen

Visbeen Associates

> "Orientation is driven by the site's offerings, views, and the path of the sun."
>
> —Wayne Visbeen

RIGHT: Designs that require moving mass quantities of dirt are often the most rewarding. With 18 rolling acres and panoramic views on the property, our team narrowed potential sites down to three and then had a fairly easy time making a decision. Figuring out how to make the design work on the chosen hilltop site was another story. The home is set on a manmade plateau at the high point of the expansive property but is worked so seamlessly into the landscape that it feels like it's always been there—site development required substantial excavation into the hillside. Indoor-outdoor living spaces were a primary design consideration. Phantom screens enclose a porch beside the patio, which is conveniently accessible from the main living space.
Photograph by William J. Hebert

PREVIOUS PAGES: Originally conceived as a Queen Anne home, the property took on a Shingle-style look with a curving hipped roof to meet the area's strict zoning requirements for height. The architecture is inspired by the past while retaining the best of the present. We were working with an imposed, maximum moveable footprint of 3,500 square feet and maximized every bit of it. The home is oriented for great morning sun in the reading loft above the foyer and unbelievable sunset views from the master bedroom, its private balcony, and its sitting room, which is uniquely expressed as a cupola. The husband and wife enjoy complete privacy as the windows in the kids' rooms face the other direction.
Photographs by Chuck Heiney

"The entrance is critical in setting the tone, but it's not just about being grand. A successful entrance is all about transition."

—Wayne Visbeen

ABOVE: The arrival experience is defined by humble yet elegant bluestone pavers—heated for wintertime convenience and safety. With the perfect setup for entertaining, a grand walkway leads from the driveway to the covered porch, which is flanked by vintage-style transom, cameo, and leaded-glass windows that add immeasurably to the ambience. The L-shaped home spans 8,000 square feet on three levels, but its façade is unpretentious, entirely welcoming. Nodding to the beautiful stone and shake houses of Europe on the exterior, the home continues a theme of Old World elegance inside with intricate paneling, moulding, and custom finishes.

FACING PAGE: Every fine detail is intentional, integrated, elegant, sophisticated. The gentle curve of the ceiling is echoed in the range hood, cabinetry, island, and furniture. Hand-hewn wood floors, fine millwork, and custom glazing techniques are thematic throughout. My team and I always applaud homeowners who prioritize rich detail ahead of square footage. It's an infinitely more challenging route, but so much greater is the reward.

Photographs by William J. Hebert

"Parameters often create answers."

—Wayne Visbeen

ABOVE: Architecture is something that can't just be talked about or scanned into a computer. Sure, we utilize computer modeling for accuracy in the construction process, but we don't go there until the look and feel has been developed. I think that sketching is the best way to initiate the design process and explain how spaces will relate to each other, work together, be finished out. To celebrate the beauty of the completed architecture, our in-house artist paints proportionately correct watercolors of all of our designs; many homeowners choose to display them quite prominently.
Rendering by David Lorenz, Visbeen Associates

FACING PAGE TOP: From the front door, you can clearly see Lake Michigan. We accomplished this welcoming transparency by placing living areas in the center of the home, where privacy isn't required. The crisp material palette and use of horizontal planes and glazing creates beautiful shadowing and a contemporary look.
Photograph by Chuck Heiney

FACING PAGE BOTTOM: Upon returning to the Midwest after traveling through Tuscany, a couple came to us with a romantic vision of an Italian villa set on an 18-acre site. The source of inspiration was clear, so we designed the home to feel like a series of small, three-story buildings with angular rooflines that intentionally read like a small village—replete with a bell tower-like form that actually houses a stairway—from a distance. Our design called for stucco, stone, and a Ludowici clay tile roof that's guaranteed for life, one of the finest in the world. The floorplan is relatively simple, extremely livable, and smartly oriented to the formal Italian garden, vineyard, reflection pond, and forested area.
Photograph by Chuck Heiney

ABOVE, LEFT, & FACING PAGE: The architecture twists and turns to capture the best views of the water on both the street-facing side and the lakefront elevation. While the plan is very open, the wings radiating from the center allow for plenty of secluded spaces. Because the home is located in a fairly traditional neighborhood, and the owners are partial to contemporary design but wanted a bit of a mountain lodge flavor, we brought together a number of seemingly disparate goals into a composition that is modern but respectful of the locale. Traditional brackets are reinterpreted as fine, tapered elements, and the use of stone and barrel-shaped forms is likewise modern. Seamless indoor-outdoor relationships and thoughtful designs like the lower-level screened-in room with fireplace and lower-level deck with summer drink bar allow the homeowners to enjoy their magnificent home and its views to the fullest all year long.
Renderings by David Lorenz, Visbeen Associates, Inc.
Photographs by Megan J. TerVeen, Visbeen Associates, Inc.

"Some architects fine-tune a style, but I think the greater challenge and reward lie in perfecting the planning process. When you understand the vocabulary of a style, no architectural genre is off limits."

—Wayne Visbeen

RIGHT & FACING PAGE: Summertime in Michigan is unparalleled—the air, the lake, the swaying dune grass, the colors—so our focus was creating a home where natural beauty could be fully enjoyed. Open yet compact, the plan gives residents a close connection to the outdoors. The top floor houses the master bedroom, the next floor—a mid-level between the main and lower level—has a generously sized patio for lounging or grilling, and the first story features direct access to the waterfront. Even with all of the glass, the house is hurricane-force ready and designed with hearty stone and cement fiber siding to survive the harshest climates. Next door to the main residence is the site's original house, which we updated for use as a guesthouse.
Photographs by William J. Hebert

Bosco Building, Inc., page 99

Easling Construction Company, page 111

structure

Bosco Building, Inc., page 99

Easling Construction Company, page 111

Bosco Building, Inc., page 99

With a rich heritage in the construction of luxurious residential properties, Bosco Building, founded by Don Bosco in 1976, is recognized as one of southeastern Michigan's most respected homebuilders. Family owned and managed, the award-winning firm has been entrusted by the most discerning clients to construct their exceptional homes.

What makes Bosco Building unique is the firm's genuine understanding and appreciation of the complexities associated with sophisticated residences. A relationship with Bosco Building begins with the initial design and continues well beyond the completion of the home. Don and his experienced team of conceptual and executive professionals devote themselves to a limited number of projects each year.

Thorough and meticulous care is taken throughout each stage of the project with particular emphasis placed on the interior finishes and detailing that truly make a house a home. This attention to the details has allowed them to collaborate with highly regarded architectural firms, talented interior designers, and skilled craftspeople.

As the market demands continue to evolve throughout southeastern Michigan, Don is focused on the implementation of new products and methods that are both sensitive to the environment and more cost effective for his clients.

"The measure of commitment is the length someone will travel to keep it."

—Don Bosco

Bosco Building, Inc.

"The selection of quality materials and depth of design vision result in residences that will stand as works of art for generations."

—Don Bosco

ABOVE: Broad expanses of lush green lawn unfurl, welcoming guests on their approach to the breathtaking neoclassical-style estate. The period-consistent use of symmetry, formal proportion, and the stately brick exterior convey classical, ageless beauty.
Photograph by Beth Singer

FACING PAGE TOP: Created with the elegance of an English cottage classic, the home sits snugly within 12 tree-shrouded acres. Visitors weave along the curves of a meandering walkway to reach the charming mahogany and beveled glass entry doors lit by authentic gas lanterns.
Photograph by George Dzahristos

FACING PAGE BOTTOM: An eclectic fusion of Victorian, Gothic, Art Deco, and Art Nouveau influences can be found throughout the home's interior, creating inviting spaces for a large family to gather. The focal point of this room is a prized circa 1923 glass lantern placed over the sitting area. The fixture, acquired years before, blends beautifully with the room's architectural details and rich mahogany tone interior.
Photograph by George Dzahristos

PREVIOUS PAGES LEFT: Designed to be the central axis to a phenomenal 10,000-square-foot home, the grand foyer leads to the formal dining room, the master suite gallery hall, the home theater, and the staircase. A handmade stained-glass dome demands attention yet creates an ethereal ambience from above, highlighting the foyer's custom Persian rug and burled walnut and ebony center table.
Photograph by George Dzahristos

PREVIOUS PAGES RIGHT: Salvaged from St. Bonaventure Church in Detroit, the circa-1883 carved oak Gothic archway serves as the focus of attention for the stunning home theater. Furnished more like a living room, the room gives a warm and comfortable impression. A convergence of Old World style with modern convenience, the space also serves as the family's central hub for security, mechanical, and interior and exterior lighting functions.
Photograph by George Dzahristos

"When building a residence, there is not a beginning or ending; it's a progressive journey of discovery."

—Don Bosco

ABOVE & FACING PAGE: Demanding a second glance, the home's ornate hand-carved front doors adorned by custom hardware make for a grand entrance into the two-and-a-half-story formal foyer space. Marble continues through the foyer into the great room, which is lined with floor-to-ceiling windows. Opulent plaster detailing accented with goldleaf complements the breathtaking dual staircase with beautifully crafted wrought-iron railing work.
Photographs by George Dzahristos

"When your house reflects your personality, you're home."

—Don Bosco

RIGHT: To incorporate the beautiful ornate antique marble fireplace into the formal dining room, we installed intricate plaster detailing and millwork. Emblazoned with goldleafing, the coved ceiling is accented with masterful crown moulding.
Photograph by George Dzahristos

FACING PAGE TOP: Elegant and inviting, the sprawling kitchen exudes a lived-in comfortable feeling through the use of warm colored materials. Accents such as painted and glazed cabinetry, traditional hardware, a natural stone backsplash, and gilded chandeliers create the impression of a habituated homey space for friends and family to gather.
Photograph by George Dzahristos

FACING PAGE BOTTOM LEFT: When working with natural products, you have to be adept at problem-solving. This space is the end result of a meticulous installation of honey onyx stone. By using both side of various slabs and a tremendous amount of patience, we painstakingly created an uninterrupted perimeter pattern down the entire length of the elongated master bath.
Photograph by George Dzahristos

FACING PAGE BOTTOM RIGHT: Stemming from the grand foyer, a layered living space shows off the collaboration of several trade professionals. The room's openness and two-foot-wide marble columns lend counterpoint to the exquisite goldleafing on the millwork and plaster detail within the crown and coved ceiling. An antique chandelier pronounces the height of the space and brings focus down to the period furniture, traditional artwork, and antique rug.
Photograph by Beth Singer

LEFT: Expansive windows in the modern dining room blur the lines between inside and out. An oval-shaped dining room table made from rosewood features a modern base of hammered steel. We wanted to take advantage of the ceiling height in the home; therefore, a tigerwood fireplace surround soars straight to the top of the 21-foot ceiling.

FACING PAGE TOP: The extensive use of limestone, cut stone, and antiqued leaded glass windows as well as a 10-foot-tall custom-made entry door lend the traditional French country home the feel of an Old World castle. Designed for entertaining, the home's majesty is reinforced by the vast reflective water feature, landscaping, and hardscaping.

FACING PAGE BOTTOM LEFT: When the client came to us to build this home, the lot was described as "interesting." Translation: challenging. Working with the architect and client, we created something unique yet organic. The essence of space, light, and materials defines a style of its own and embraces the location instead of fighting it.

FACING PAGE BOTTOM RIGHT: Fieldstone columns rise from the natural wood-burning fireplace with custom flue, bridging the room's living space to the open cathedral ceiling and geometric skylights. Large expanses of exterior walls are radiused with bent glass windows yielding 180 degrees of breathtaking views.
Photographs by Beth Singer

"Grand-scale projects require the talents of many to seamlessly weave together, and when it all comes together, magic happens."

—Don Bosco

ABOVE: A circular driveway frames the center courtyard and fountain leading to the solid limestone steps of the regal estate residence. Antiqued milk glass windows, used as an architectural element, allow light into the home while restoring privacy. A blending of various traditional materials creates a statuesque and dramatic foreshadowing of what is to be discovered inside.

FACING PAGE: For the focal point of the stunning traditional library, we incorporated a reclaimed European mantel into the custom millwork. The rich tones of mahogany paneling, millwork, and coffered ceiling bordered with reclaimed tin accentuate the antiqued leaded glass windows.
Photographs by Beth Singer

It might seem a bit unusual for the proprietor of an acclaimed construction firm to live in a century-old farmhouse rather than a home he built with his own two hands. But the man loves home improvement projects, making every element the best it can be, and those historic walls have proven an excellent canvas for renovations, additions, and alterations of all sorts. Being his own client has given Marty Easling a great understanding of what it's like to be the client; those who commission him appreciate his well-rounded perspective. A graduate of Michigan Technological University with a degree in civil engineering, Marty has mastered the art of working with people and their plans. He surpasses his clients' expectations.

Marty's team is a hundred strong, and many of his artisans and craftsmen have been with him for decades; they like complex projects, and Marty's architect colleagues more than deliver the challenges. Concrete, masonry, rough and finish carpentry, insulation, roofing, drywall hanging and finishing, hardwood floors, ceramic tile, cabinetry, painting—nothing is out of their realm of expertise. Though Marty has this great team of professionals, he personally visits every jobsite every day, and even after projects are complete, he continues his relationship with clients and their homes through his firm's Home Maintenance Division. His subsequent commissions, remodels, and additions are a credit to the team's commitment to quality and service.

"It's a welcome challenge to create a home that matches the beauty of nature."

—Marty Easling

Easling Construction Company

"Choosing a palette of natural materials is the best way to lend instant authenticity to a space."

—Marty Easling

LEFT & PREVIOUS PAGES: Working with Lou DesRosier's design, the future residents, and a sizeable lakefront lot, we built the home from the ground up. To create a smooth indoor-outdoor connection, we incorporated a 54-foot-wide, tempered glass wall and plenty of natural materials. The exterior is clad in western red cedar, the fireplace is done with local fieldstone, and the floors are maple. The aesthetic is really clean, contemporary, and easy going. The complex framing is hidden by load-bearing columns lining the perimeter of the interior.
Photographs by Bruce Buck

ABOVE: The open layout—dining room, living room, office, and kitchen—is perfect for entertaining friends and family, but because the home has an inviting ambience, it's just as appealing for a party of one or two. The Idaho flagstone patio stays cool all year long, but the interior's radiant-heated floors ensure that the owners can comfortably walk around barefoot in the middle of winter. Likewise, the large skylight brings in natural light to visually warm the space.

FACING PAGE TOP: The master bedroom's private, 16-foot-wide balcony is accessed via a pair of cleverly shaped doors that we crafted at our millwork shop. The home faces sunset west, and the design really accentuates the views.

FACING PAGE BOTTOM: Custom cabinetry, wall paneling, and 1-by-4 V-groove paneling set a clean contemporary aesthetic. The lighting scheme creates interest and drama for the otherwise neutral canvas.
Photographs by Bruce Buck

"Selecting the right wood is critical to integrating the elements of a forest setting while maintaining the integrity of the home's style."

—Marty Easling

ABOVE: The condo overlooks the Boardman River in downtown Traverse City. The more contemporary look is accomplished with the smooth finishing details of cherry. We carefully selected "all heart" cherry, eliminating sapwood and knots. The grain of the cherry flows cleanly from floor to walls with endmatched boards for a more refined look.
Photograph by James Yochum Photography

RIGHT: The clean simple lines of the cherry extend into the master bedroom. The cherry carries a natural finish to develop the soft patina of the wood. This balance works throughout the home with its sharp vertical and horizontal breaks.
Photograph by James Yochum Photography

FACING PAGE TOP: A traditional Northern Michigan cottage focuses on its woodwork. The glowing finish on the wood in the stairwell accents the knotty pine walls, Douglas fir balustrades and newel posts, and the eastern white pine floor. The warmth of the wood interior encourages relaxation in all seasons.
Photograph by Peter Tata Photography

FACING PAGE BOTTOM: The porch overlooking the beach is the central "up north" gathering place. Here, we continued the varied wood combinations with mahogany decking chosen for the floor and a Douglas fir beaded ceiling. Today's cottage look is updated with white painted trim. The contrast of geometric columns and railing mirroring the door and window designs frames the foliage along the lake.
Photograph by Peter Tata Photography

"Anybody can build a house. It takes real talent and a lot of creative collaboration to build a home."

—Marty Easling

ABOVE & FACING PAGE: Home placement is a detail that is critical. Nestling this home in the mature trees and facing due south on Big Glen Lake allows the owners to make good use of their varied and plentiful outdoor leisure spaces. Comfortable in all seasons, the interior and exterior views are incredible.
Photographs by James Yochum Photography

"There are so many great materials out there, but it's important to exercise restraint when specifying them: If you get too many in the mix, it will look forced, unnatural."

—Marty Easling

LEFT: The master bedroom of a Grand Traverse Bay home features a great patio that follows the shape of the breakfast nook's bay window on the lower level. The cedar shingles and white trim detailing create a simple yet elegant look, putting the focus on the beautiful natural surroundings.

FACING PAGE: Located on Big Glen Lake, the home boasts five fireplaces—building this home was a fun challenge. The patio's wood-burning fireplace is 22 feet tall and clad in Michigan fieldstone. The stone was split and chiseled onsite to keep the mortar joints to a minimum and the width uniform for a polished and professionally executed appearance. The Douglas fir pergola that our team of artisans constructed is complementary in form and height to the outdoor fireplace.
Photographs by James Yochum Photography

"Partnering with a client to build a house is often the start of a lifelong relationship. Both are equally important."

—Dan Sebold

elements of structure

There is no substitute for a half century of building experience. Founded in 1955 by architect Thomas Sebold, Thomas Sebold & Associates gradually shifted its focus from design to construction. As a trusted partner to world-renowned architects such as Minoru Yamasaki and Hugh Newell Jacobsen, Thomas quickly established TSA's position in the luxury home market. Building on that legacy, president Dan Sebold and vice president Glenn Kunnath have developed a team of talented and professional craftsmen whose pride is evident in every project they undertake. TSA's longstanding commitment to quality and craftsmanship has secured the firm a preeminent position in the Michigan building market.

Dan and Glenn, along with a dedicated group of construction professionals, are involved in each phase of the building process, from design and value engineering to execution. This ensures a build that is fiscally and structurally sound. Thomas Sebold & Associates' highly skilled group of carpenters routinely create woodworking masterpieces to accompany residential or commercial projects. This capability has become a prized partner for many top design professionals and homeowners alike. While TSA is best known for custom residential work, historic restoration, commercial projects, estate management, and green building are vital parts of its repertoire.

Thomas Sebold & Associates

RIGHT & PREVIOUS PAGES: The regal French Tudor estate presides over an equally manicured landscape. In an effort to incorporate the rolling landscape, several layers of natural stone were used to both highlight and divide the greenery. The interplay of the grounds, created by CHS Land Design, and the estate, designed by Young & Young Architects, brings balance and historical authenticity to the home. In front, the semicircular residence frames the sweeping arrival courtyard. Guests are ushered in to the private, formal courtyard by a limestone porte-cochère, which also houses the well-appointed guest suite. Here again, natural elements such as stone and shrubbery are shaped by master craftsmen to create the balance and order of a historic estate. Collaborating with the best tradespeople, incorporating the latest advances in building technology, and practicing time-honored methods of craftsmanship lead to timeless architecture. This theme is repeated inside with the luxurious designs of Ausburg Interiors.
Photographs by Jim Haefner

ABOVE & FACING PAGE: The one-of-a-kind wrought-iron pergola was created to be the focal point of the upper-level terrace. The pergola's glass floor acts as a skylight for the indoor pool below. Due to the complexity and sophistication of the pool room's ceiling vaults, concrete forms were erected in place to ensure perfect symmetry and fit. The neutral palette of the marble columns, limestone walls and floor, and cast concrete ceiling highlights each texture and defines the crisp blue and unique shape of the pool. The elaborate glass tile mosaic at the center of the pool further highlights the contrast between the stone and water elements.
Photographs by Jim Haefner

"The clean lines of a contemporary home mask the complexities involved in the design, layout, and execution."

—Dan Sebold

ABOVE & FACING PAGE: The clean lines and lack of ornamentation in a contemporary home mask the complexities involved in the design, layout, and execution. Without layers of detailing, craftsmanship and precision are on full display. Horizontal moulding details often run from room to room, creating a continuous line throughout the home. For the home on Cass Lake, designed by AZD Associates, large sections of glass were a must to take full advantage of the water views.
Photographs by Beth Singer

ABOVE LEFT: Glass is used as a primary material to provide open interior spaces with unobstructed views of the water. Throughout all three stories, metal, stone, wood, and glass are used in various combinations to create visual interest and unique installations. The main staircase serves as a focal point of the front entry, an engineering marvel, and a work of art. By piercing the structural glass wall with stair treads, the weight of the stairs is carried by an invisible wall, creating the illusion of a floating staircase.

ABOVE RIGHT: The combination of natural materials and sophisticated design is a prominent theme throughout the residence.

FACING PAGE TOP: Each element was handmade, from the exotic veneers on the cabinet doors and drawer fronts to the custom pullouts and storage units to the countertop and island. The kitchen is tailored to meet the homeowners' every need.

FACING PAGE BOTTOM: The glass bridge joins private and public sides of the atrium and overlooks the custom fireplace surround. Its curved form stands in sharp contrast to the straight lines and precise geometry of the rest of the residence.
Photographs by Beth Singer

ABOVE: The architecture of McIntosh Poris Associates masterfully complements the site's atypical triangular shape. With a humble one-story presentation on the street side, the house expands dramatically to take advantage of the mature forest behind. The master suite and entertaining spaces reside on the main floor, taking full advantage of the large expanse of windows. The home's lower level boasts a fitness center complete with sauna and multiple guestrooms.

FACING PAGE: Balanced against the formal, Zen-like exterior, the interior is composed of informal, open space. Designer Kevin McManamon's use of symmetrical layouts punctuated with organic shapes and natural materials continues the exterior's theme of sculpted natural beauty. This creates a clear, unified aesthetic for the home.
Photographs by Kevin Bauman

ABOVE & FACING PAGE: At the touch of a button, a glass door slides away to welcome home a 40-foot yacht. Although engineering a home that straddles the shoreline was a daunting task, entering the exclusive fraternity of builders who have accomplished this feat was well worth it. The Bay Harbor Marina property designed by Young & Young Architects takes full advantage of the spectacular views by allowing the residents a 180-degree sightline from the three-story turret. The generous amount of expertly installed curved millwork and mouldings, as well as the custom cabinetry and built-ins, designed by Pace Interiors, are as impressive as the lake views that they frame.
Photographs by Gene Meadows

Arcways

Neenah, Wisconsin

"When the craftsmen control every aspect of the project—from design to installation—the outcome is flawless."

—Tom Stilp

ABOVE: Contrasts can make the strongest statements; we used travertine for the stairway's body, cherry on the side stringers, and forged iron balustrades—all set against a black walnut floor. The mixture of ferrous and nonferrous elements makes a dramatic statement.

FACING PAGE: For a home with large, competing features, we wanted to make sure the stairway maintained its presence. We designed and constructed a massive bowed and flared bottom to offer the correct proportions. The starting newel posts and open riser add to a rustic, reclaimed feel and work well in a post-and-beam or cabin-style home.
Photographs courtesy of Arcways Stairways

"You should always be able to rely on the judgment of the professionals you're working with. Otherwise, you're working with the wrong professionals."

—Tom Stilp

ABOVE: We love a challenge, and a complex design layout gave us just that. The 14-foot bottom mirrors the balcony treatment to balance the entryway at its centerline. Perfectly detailed with brass and verdigris, the custom forged iron railing flows through the midlanding space.

FACING PAGE: Trusting our expertise from 45 years of experience, the homeowner decided to go with gilded wood balusters as opposed to iron panels. From the marble floors to the Spain-imported balusters, the rich details play off of one another to create a stunning, pristine foyer.
Photographs courtesy of Arcways Stairways

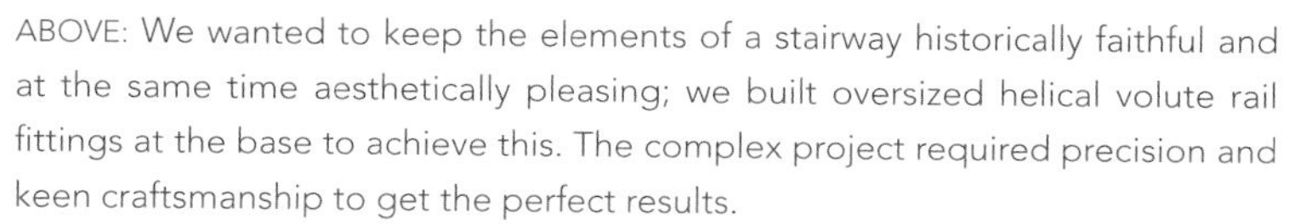

ABOVE: We wanted to keep the elements of a stairway historically faithful and at the same time aesthetically pleasing; we built oversized helical volute rail fittings at the base to achieve this. The complex project required precision and keen craftsmanship to get the perfect results.

FACING PAGE: To maintain a warm elegance, we juxtaposed carved wood newel post beginnings with iron panels and wood top rails. The custom-forged iron balustrade with wood-panelized side face creates a seamless visual flow that keeps with the graceful design.
Photographs courtesy of Arcways Stairways

"Seeing the intense amount of work—engineering, artistry, and craftsmanship—that goes into a stairway is something you never forget."

—Tom Stilp

ABOVE LEFT: Achieving a modern look without appearing too cold can be tricky, but we used wood and glass barrels to anchor the beginning of the stairway, offering warmth and personality. The use of sap maple contrasted with the glass panels added to the effect.

ABOVE RIGHT: Precisely matching the grain and color of the sapele mahogany wood stair components is a highly involved process—but the results are well worth the investment. The bookmatched wood on the sides of the stairway nicely complements the modern interior.

FACING PAGE TOP: Complex and stunning, the design for integrating a companion elevator into a three-floor stacked stairway includes simple lines in a flat radius; the contrast was achieved through mixing black walnut and stained white oak.

FACING PAGE BOTTOM: The interior radius for the stairway's midpoint was extreme; we carefully crafted the tightness of the curves for precision. From the foyer, the stairs offer a lasting first impression with the flared and bowed base and helical barrel beginnings. Rich black walnut with a rubbed-bronze forged iron finish adds to the striking appearance.

Photographs courtesy of Arcways Stairway

Grabill Windows & Doors

Almont, Michigan

"Every project reveals the generations of craftsmanship that came before it. Tradition, skill, and technique carry on."

—Teresa Grabill

ABOVE & FACING PAGE: Our product line can fulfill any project parameters, including oversized and irregular shaped windows and doors. We used American black walnut with bronze cladding to create NFRC-certified, high-performance fixed-in-frame windows, lift-and-slide doors, and exterior folding door units.
Photographs by The Aspen Marketing Group

"A craftsman can't be willing to sacrifice any components of his trade. Aesthetics, practicality, technology—they're all imperative."

—Greg Grabill

ABOVE & FACING PAGE: Often times, our projects include a variety of elements; we collaborate with the architects and designers to make sure everything is perfect. Irregular and oversized fixed-in-frame windows, fixed and motorized operable clerestory windows, exterior folding doors, and an offset pivot door serve very different purposes yet come together for a stunning overall look. American black walnut interior elements cast a welcome warmth, while the heavy-gauge bronze cladding provides Old World protection from the elements.
Photographs by The Aspen Marketing Group

"There is no substitute for trust in building relationships and no substitute for sound woodworking and business practices in building trust."

—Phillip Kline

ABOVE & RIGHT: Contemporary oversized mahogany, corner-glazed, fixed-in-frame windows are as beautiful as they are efficient. Custom hardware and finishes complete the project.
Photographs by George Dzahristos

FACING PAGE: Everything is custom, which means we have few limitations. For a distinct, one-of-a-kind Asian retreat, we created mahogany lifts and slide Shoji doors, as well as fixed windows and interior Shoji screen doors. The homeowners loved our ability to offer singular, unique products to their house.
Photographs by Wujcik Construction Group, Inc

LEFT & FACING PAGE: Our detailed eye and careful engineering made mahogany out-swing casement windows with true divided lights, in-swing doors, fixed doors, and clerestory windows work perfectly. Function is as critical as form.
Photographs by Beth Singer

MOD Interiors

Ira Township, Michigan

"Wood is one of the greatest natural materials in the world. Like people and fingerprints, no two are the same."

—Matthew Gaglio

ABOVE: To gain ultimate climate control for the wine room behind the table and chairs, we used triple thermal-glazed glass and tight weather seals on all sides of the solid walnut doors. Using templates, we fabricated the entire opening offsite and installed it to conform to the barrel ceiling.

FACING PAGE: We used a multitude of different materials to achieve the room's lavish ambience. We laid out and installed the Old World tin ceiling to keep even perimeter margins between ceiling curves and edges of the tin panel pattern. We conformed the mouldings, custom antique mirrors, and silverleafed frames to the shapes of the curved arches. The bar front consists of quartersawn white oak with an antique lime finish. For a feel of age and authenticity, we installed a zinc bar top, a popular feature of old English and Irish pubs.
Photographs by George Dzahristos

"There are thousands of wood species—all with their own character and texture—that can be shaped, carved, or bent into most any form. The only limit is your imagination."

—Matthew Gaglio

ABOVE & FACING PAGE: For consistency in the color, grain, and character of the wood, we selected and used a single quartersawn walnut tree for the cognac room. Each panel has two veneer leaves with a center-balanced seam. Walnut lumber has a large natural variation in color, and we ordered twice what we needed and, with the architect, sorted the material for color and character and arranged the selected groups consistently throughout the house.
Photographs by George Dzahristos

SCENIC WONDERS OF AMERICA
We Americans

"Finely crafted woodwork can be appreciated and enjoyed beyond its natural surroundings."

—Matthew Gaglio

ABOVE: For convenience and visual appeal, all panels between the display and book shelves are cabinet doors on touch latches. So that the paneling is not cluttered with plugs and switches, each room has one control panel for lighting, audio, video, and security—their locations laid out in the early stages of construction so they would be centered between panel rails. Poplar columns and the overhead beam frame the entrance to the room.

FACING PAGE: Employing an extensive and meticulous process, we fumed all of the riftsawn white oak woodwork. Due to the openness of the room and the high concentrations of ammonia that are required for fuming, we fabricated all components offsite and arranged them methodically on racks in a large sealed space so that air could flow around each piece evenly. Everything had to be perfect.

Photographs by George Dzahristos

"There's a great sense of satisfaction that comes from taking a raw piece of material and creating something that will be around for generations to come."

—Matthew Gaglio

TOP: For consistency, we used wood from the same tree throughout both rooms. The sliding wall separating them appears as one continuous wall when in the closed position, and we took great efforts to seamlessly conceal the panel track within the crown moulding and fixed panels. As craftsmen who work with, revere, and hold the ultimate respect for natural materials, we've been involved with a great deal of sustainable, environmentally responsible projects.
Photograph courtesy of Neumann/Smith Architecture

MIDDLE & BOTTOM: We built the massive display system offsite and assembled it onsite to appear as one continuous unit wrapping around doorways and opening into other rooms. It spans more than 40 feet of walls from ceiling to floor and required 50 sheets of maple veneered panels, which we treated with yellow aniline dye and then finally toned to make up for natural variations in the wood.
Photographs by Justin Maconochie, Korab/Hedrich Blessing Photography

FACING PAGE: Consisting of solid white oak with a large complex curved cornice and matching copper wire mesh display doors, the china cabinet's light color and antique, limed finish whimsically contrast the vermillion gloss finish of the entry doors.
Photograph by George Dzahristos

PARTANS
JOHNSON
33

Glass Tek

Metamora, Michigan

"Glass never seems dated. It is timeless, always looking fresh and new and clean. That's why people do much more with it now than ever."

—Tod Caron

ABOVE: In the home's grand foyer, we built the skylight but had to accommodate the chandelier, which is hooked up to a wench and pulley system so that it can be lowered 40 feet to ground level for cleaning. We designed and built the structural steel of the skylight as well as the glass and the copper finish on the outside. Despite the skepticism of many, we found a way to make this design work.
Photograph by James Haefner

FACING PAGE: Working with the architect from napkin drawings to completion, we built the brushed stainless-steel supports for the marble leaning bar as well as the television surround. Backpainted green glass squares line the bar's display portals while the tempered glass trophy shelves on stainless-steel posts—milled so that there are no mounting tabs or exposed fasteners—appear to be floating.
Photograph by George Dzahristos

"The challenge of taking on difficult tasks allows for projects that are different, unique, and rewarding—we never do the same thing twice."

—Tod Caron

ABOVE: So that the shower walls would not have any brackets holding it together, we imbedded the glass walls into the floor and wall slate as well as the ceiling. Special bracketry and holes in the glass allow for the bench to pass through. Instead of using channels or clamps, we glued the panels together with structural silicone.
Photograph by George Dzahristos

FACING PAGE TOP: To fit the contours of the sky bridge's curved glass—which are among the bigger glass floor panels that have been installed in Michigan to date—we had to curve the steel offsite then weld it into place. We covered the structural steel in automotive body filler, sanded it smooth, and painted it with automotive paint to give it the sheen of artwork—a simultaneously exposed and refined design element.
Photograph courtesy of Glass Tek

FACING PAGE BOTTOM: When other glass companies told the architect the shower couldn't be constructed the way it was drawn, we proved them wrong. It took six people to carry the glass and stand it upright. A stainless frame borders the floating backlit mirror.
Photograph by Kevin Bauman

"It is important to inspire individual choice while still honing a vision."

—Cheryl Nestro

elements of design

Working from her renovated studio, Tutto Interiors' founder Cheryl Nestro is inspired by her surroundings. The space Cheryl was working in for five years had a facelift that was great, until she discovered a historic gem in 2008. She transformed the 100-year-old space, retaining its architectural bones, wide plank flooring, tin ceilings, and exposed brick walls. She knocked out walls, added innovative lighting, and repainted the rooms. Cheryl integrated a glass-enclosed office and turned laminate cabinetry into metallic-painted elegance with oversized hardware. The multifaceted designer has created a treasure-box atelier replete with jeweled chandeliers and beautiful vignettes. "My studio is so inviting, meeting with homeowners here sparks the creative process," says Cheryl.

While Cheryl was renovating an aging residence, she discovered her passion for interior design and its transformative power. Cheryl guides her clientele to an understanding of their personal style while opening up possibilities and inspiring individual choice. Specializing in transitional and traditional interiors, she masterfully interprets the dreams of discerning homeowners. Her eclectic, full-service design studio offers everything pertinent to the design process for a single room to a new home construction. Cheryl's design expertise is evident in her award-winning custom home interiors. Her work is well published, and she has been acknowledged in *Visions of Design* as one of North America's top interior designers.

Tutto Interiors

"Seeing a vision come to life is the most rewarding."

—Cheryl Nestro

ABOVE & FACING PAGE: My design vision for understated wall and window treatments uses a unified family of fabrics and colors to create an elegant backdrop without overpowering the space. I integrated transitional sofas for a clean look that updates an otherwise traditional theme. For the bay window, I designed luxurious silk drapery panels hung on decorative rods above the bay to create an illusion of higher ceilings.

PREVIOUS PAGES: We transformed an outdated room with harsh white walls and trim into a subdued, multi-layered haven featuring an impressive Habersham Belmont library system media center with combination finishes, sized to fit the eight-foot ceilings of the 1960s-era home. Glazed, rustic earth-tones combine to create a warm and inviting space, perfectly faux-aged for fine furnishings.
Photographs by Beth Singer

"The beauty of design is to deliver the imaginable."

—Cheryl Nestro

LEFT: The powder room has Old World ambience inspired by the gilded Baroque-style mirror. Marble tile wainscoting rises to 52 inches high, appropriate to the room's 10-foot ceilings; crown mouldings are nonexistent so the large mirror is center stage. I designed a concrete vanity with sculptural scrollwork to introduce a surprise element of enduring quality. Artfully patinated walls give an air of antiquity to the new home.

FACING PAGE: Formal Schonbek chandeliers with a drizzle of amber-hued crystals light the way from the grand foyer up the winding staircase. I recommended the champagne Lusterstone wall treatment with a bas-relief lace effect, extending the same color tone in every room. The owners fell in love with the 1883 Louis XVI mirror sourced from HorseFeathers Home of Toronto; it leans majestically in the entrance hall. Niches in the dining room have a soft Lusterstone finish for dramatic contrast to the dark wood buffet. In the music conservatory-reading room, we designed a fireplace to echo the rich finish of the Habersham Belmont library system.
Photographs by Don Kurek Photography

"The most successful spaces strike a delicate balance between classical and modern style."

—Cheryl Nestro

ABOVE: I persuaded the owners to use slate tile as an ideal material to underscore the wet bar focal point. Opalescent mosaic tile underneath the cabinetry adds a beautiful shimmer to the space. Because the Habersham Trevi media center dominates the space, I carefully selected fabrics and furnishings to balance the room in terms of color and scale.

FACING PAGE: I discovered some antique six-inch-square handmade tiles with the intention of using them in my own studio. A homeowner saw the tile and loved the Art Deco influence—and we decided to incorporate it into her new home. The bathroom suite was the perfect place for the artisan tile. Its muted tones inspired the idea of natural blue-grey slate flooring and walls. The hand-painted Peruvian bombe vanity and contemporary Schonbek Geometrix pendant lights are the perfect appointments.
Photographs by Don Kurek Photography

"All aspects of the design process include balance."

—Cheryl Nestro

LEFT & FACING PAGE: Symmetry commands attention in the transitional room design, so I chose a pair of demilune commodes of French neoclassical style to flank the fireplace. The commodes have inlaid leather tops and gilded tooling above each drawer. The homeowners wanted to avoid oversized or overstuffed furnishings, so I selected the Hickory Chair sofa for its clean lines. The renovation required all new furnishings from accessories to flooring, wall colors to window treatments. Forest green tiles on the fireplace surround were replaced with tumbled stone tile and glass Deco dot accents. We refreshed an old wooden fireplace mantel by hand-coating it with Techstone to appear like carved French limestone.
Photographs by Don Kurek Photography

"The beauty of great design is apparent in every detail."

—Cheryl Nestro

ABOVE: I refreshed a very traditional dining room for today's lifestyle. The table design combines unexpected colors and finishes: A rustic ebonized base contrasts the light French grey linen surface. I married Chippendale armchairs with more contemporary side chairs from Hickory Chair to streamline the ensemble. The functional sideboard has chunky metal hardware for a decidedly modern touch. A magnificent Shonbek crystal chandelier illuminates while the subtle paisley rug unifies the sophisticated space.

FACING PAGE: I updated the drab 1980s living room into a comfortably elegant space. My transitional makeover features coffered ceilings painted crisp white on taupe to highlight the room's architectural element. The big challenge was to design tailored window treatments: My unconventional approach layered pleated fabric valances behind full-length drapery panels to frame the windows beautifully. A Persian rug anchors the room with its classic flowering pattern. Warm, gold-toned walls provide a perfect foil for custom furniture and leather chairs, making the room fit for 21st-century lounging.
Photographs by Don Kurek Photography

Jean Stoffer Design

River Forest, Illinois

"The kitchen is the social core of the home. It needs to be visually interesting, warm, inviting, and above all, functional."

—Jean Stoffer

ABOVE & FACING PAGE: We strive to create classic kitchens with a fresh twist. Our simple, yet elegant look integrates architectural elements found elsewhere in the home. In the remodeled kitchen, we added classic crown mouldings, several windows for a sparkling interplay of light, and an arched cooking alcove to reference the home's architectural aesthetic. Textured ceramic tile has a watercolor glaze which is visually interesting in its subtlety. Ebonized wood and polished Calcutta marble run counterpoint to white built-in cabinetry while the modernity of a full integrated stainless-steel counter and sink juxtapose nicely with the warmth of traditional cabinetry.
Photographs by John Stoffer

"The visual elements of a home's architecture can become inspiration for kitchen design."

—Jean Stoffer

ABOVE & FACING PAGE: The residence's historic Spanish architecture and a client's love of Mexico influenced my colorful, layered design. Soltiel floor tile was laid in an interesting pattern while mesquite wood was carved for unique window lentils; many artifacts and decorative objects were collected to bring the ambience and vitality of Mexico into the space. Rustic wrought-iron light fixtures, a magnificent walnut island countertop, hammered copper sinks, and turquoise glazed ceramic tiles blend to form an exciting Mexican-Spanish vibe. Architectural elements include built-in niches and stone-faced alcoves to define work and storage areas with panache.
Photographs by John Stoffer

"I enjoy applying classic design in a modern context."

—Jean Stoffer

RIGHT & FACING PAGE: We designed the kitchen of an 1872 Victorian jewel to be architecturally in sync with the home. The Victorian vernacular is typically imbued with dark woods and heavy ornamentation, but we used a more winsome approach of pared-down decorative details and lighter finishes while keeping the same proportions and forms that resonate with the style. We found an antique wood cupboard with float glass doors and combined it with a custom wood range hood that was made to look like the same vintage. The turned legs of the island reference Victorian farm tables of old but provide modern function by maintaining a height perfect for food preparation. A classic sink stand belies the sleek European dishwasher hiding behind the cabinetry. We have mastered the fine art of seamlessly integrating modern lifestyle kitchens and their technology with the vintage homes that host them.

Photographs by John Stoffer

"An eclectic design approach makes a kitchen visually interesting. Using multiple materials in subtle tones gives depth and richness to a space."

—Jean Stoffer

ABOVE: The homeowners wanted their kitchen to feel fresh and provide a welcoming backdrop for family and friends. We combined elements, shapes and forms that are classic and restrained. Nickel lighting fixtures in modern conical shapes complement the polished granite island and black soapstone countertops. Dark walnut, honey maple, white-painted wood cabinetry, and oak flooring work together in harmony. An impressive built-in unit conceals the refrigerator, freezer, and fabulous gourmet coffee center. Above the Wolf range, we hid the exhaust hood with a fireplace mantel for a beautiful effect. We chose beadboard and elongated subway tiles to create a uniquely subtle backsplash.

FACING PAGE: Bare windows allow glowing light into the soft and elegant space. The room's open flow is ideal for family gatherings while the work island offers a durable surface for practical food preparation and has plenty of storage space. Distinctive cabinetry hardware of nickel and pewter coexists alongside an English-inspired fireclay apron front sink.
Photographs by John Stoffer

W•D Flooring

Laona, Wisconsin

"Operating for sustainability is a sentiment we don't take lightly."

—Peter Connor

ABOVE: Contrary to popular belief, American forest growth exceeds harvest by almost 50 percent. Because we've been in the industry for more than a century, we know that protecting this statistic is critical. Located in Wisconsin, our timberland consists of sustainable forests; we use a rotating, 40,000-acre stock.
Photograph courtesy of W•D Flooring

FACING PAGE: Contrast has a powerful effect on a space. To offset the riftsawn white oak on the walls of a home designed by Domain Architecture, we used dark walnut on the floor as well as for the island paneling.
Photograph by Gallop Studio

"Diversity of species and product choices—that's our concentration."

—Peter Connor

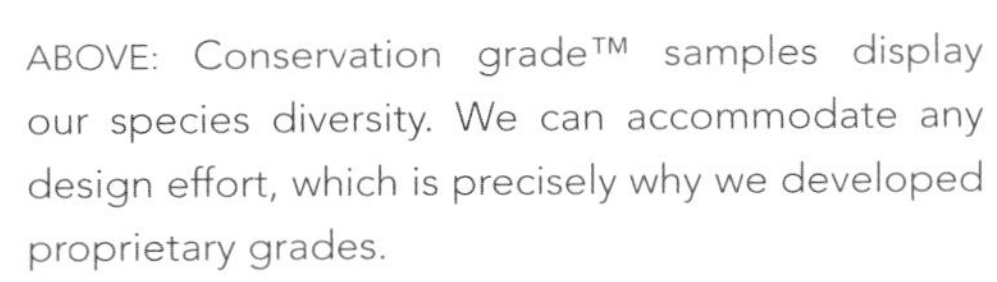

ABOVE: Conservation grade™ samples display our species diversity. We can accommodate any design effort, which is precisely why we developed proprietary grades.
Photographs courtesy of W•D Flooring

FACING PAGE TOP: Our conservation grade™ maple gives a warm feel to a modern loft concept in the Bridgewater Condominiums in Minneapolis.
Photograph by Gallop Studio

FACING PAGE BOTTOM: For an office setting, we took an unexpected cue from the planks of a ship deck. Multiple species come together to create the bold statement: stained ebony ash and pickled white maple make up the flooring.
Photograph by Gallop Studio

RIGHT: FSC™ maple adds to the transparent design of a Charles Stinson stairwell.
Photograph courtesy of Charles R. Stinson Architects

FACING PAGE TOP: When we built an FSC™-certified home that required 100-percent eco-friendly materials, we explored all of our options. An FSC™ conservation grade™ floor conveys all of the advantages of a traditional hard maple floor but has a modern edge to it. The duality of classic versus contemporary is clear.
Photograph courtesy of Charles R. Stinson Architects

FACING PAGE BOTTOM: A green house doesn't have to sacrifice elegance. We helped prove it with a Keith Waters and Associates Ideas home, rated by Minnesota Green Star. Traditional with all modern updates, the rooms use FSC™ conservation grade™ flooring in red birch.
Photographs by LandMark Photograph

"W.D. Connor led in the concept of sustainable forestry in the early 20th century. We're just carrying on the tradition."

—Peter Connor

ABOVE: Without the walnut floors and clean woodwork, the room of a private residence would have a completely different feel. Our work offers simple elegance.

FACING PAGE: In the MacPhail Music School's great hall, we worked with James Dayton Designs. Our goal was to frame the room without overshadowing the performance area. Edge grain maple sets off the Douglas fir paneling. The floor shows clean lines with the wood grain running tangential to the face, minimizing any possible figuring.
Photographs by Gallop Studio

STEINWAY & SONS

Atelier Lapchi

Chicago, Illinois

"The perfect carpet expresses who we are and what we love: the colors, textures, and patterns that we find engaging and inspiring."

—Kerry Smith

ABOVE: Lapchi hand weaves carpets of exceptional beauty and ecological integrity. Lanolin-rich Himalayan wools and fine silks are dyed, spun, carded, woven, and finished entirely by the hands of Nepali artisans. These beautiful natural materials are tinted with eco-friendly dyes and require no harsh chemicals or finishes that might injure the breathtaking beauty of the Kathmandu valley or its people. While preserving an ancient art form, we also support GoodWeave, which means that our carpets are artful expressions of child-free, fair labor practice.
Photograph by Michael Jones

FACING PAGE: We have developed an extensive library of designs that can be customized in color, fiber, scale, pile height, and finish. It is rewarding to collaborate with interior designers and their clients to realize a vision—or to develop one—though many people find their perfect rug in the abundant variety of our showroom. It's all about line, form, and color. The Lapchi pattern library reflects a wide span of influence—echoes from thousands of years ago and provocative contemporary abstractions alike—and each motif has a story to tell. It's this level of thought and detail that defines all of our rugs, whether custom or tailor made from our collection.
Photograph by Nathan Kirkman

"Partnering with GoodWeave is part of our ongoing commitment to make each carpet an aesthetically special and socially responsible choice."

—Kerry Smith

ABOVE LEFT: Based on a French Deco silk in the African style, Chevron celebrates its exotic parentage by spiraling sensuously over the carpet surface. Its undulating movement creates a pattern that adapts easily to all furniture groupings and possibilities.

ABOVE RIGHT: An essay in mark making, Etched recalls the painstaking artistic technique wielded by master artists Rembrandt and Van Dyke and turns it into a new kind of luxury surface for the art of living. The simple repeating element creates a rhythmic surface of sophisticated flexibility.

FACING PAGE: Like deep space images seen though the Hubble telescope, Nebulous speaks of patterns that have no solid form but possess a moody presence, mystery, and elegance. As spatially evocative and abstract as a contemporary painting, Nebulous is fine art for the floor.

Photographs by Michael Jones

"Participating in the design of a custom carpet is very exciting; the result is a foundation in perfect harmony with its environment."

—Kerry Smith

TOP: "Satori" is the moment of sudden enlightenment in Zen practice. Our Satori rug epitomizes the international interests and passions of the 18th-century enlightened view of the world. Its blossom-filled tendrils capture the cross-cultural fusion of East and West and the peaceful garden of the enlightened mind.

MIDDLE: Arrowroot echoes the fabled furnishings of Ming Dynasty China, where refined artistic connoisseurship was at its peak. The rug's spiraling vines and broad clustered leaves invite the eye to wander along its slender stalks.

BOTTOM: A lyrical trellis of leaves, tendrils, and dew-frosted pomegranates, Thalia pays homage to the nature-inspired visions of the Arts-and-Crafts movement and Japan's floating world. Celebrating the gentle beauty of silhouetted shapes and naturalistic details, Thalia is simple, timeless, and elegant.

FACING PAGE: Emerging from prewar Europe, the pattern of Meadow is at the cusp of traditional representation and geometric modernity. Bold shapes bloom across the carpet surface, looking at once naive and sophisticated, playful and restrained.
Photographs by Michael Jones

Vogue Furniture

Royal Oak, Michigan

"Great modern design can best be achieved by maintaining symmetry and simplicity."

—Greg Bartelt

ABOVE: With a naturally occurring array of black, red, and gold, macassar ebony wall panels incorporate hidden storage. The bar and dining table in sapele with solid bronze inlays and border—as well as a sofa table in burled walnut—masterfully complement the modern design of the living space. Interior design by Eric Charles Interiors. Architecture by Irving Tobocman.

FACING PAGE: Creating warmth and dimension, expansive satinwood wall paneling with horizontal and vertical delineations conceals storage. The geometric pattern and blending of walls with rug accentuate the shape of the corridor, an effective introduction to the family space of the home.
Photographs by Beth Singer

"It's much easier to design in a space that has challenges—the room itself makes a lot of the decisions."

—Greg Bartelt

ABOVE: We designed and paneled the entire room in solid mahogany with bookmatched and sequenced veneer wall panels. Floor-to-ceiling pilasters create strong vertical lines, drawing deserved attention to the room's high ceiling and open space. Interior design by Kevin McManamon.
Photograph by Beth Singer

FACING PAGE TOP: In a simple and contemporary environment, clean lines and sharp contrasts highlight the dramatic panoramic mountain vista. We used bookmatched ribbon sapele for the dining table and stained the buffet and lower cabinetry to blend with rustic timbers. Satin lacquer upper cabinetry with a stainless-steel appliance wall and backsplash adds a further touch of modern elegance. Interior design by Schaerer Architextural Interiors.
Photographs by Shawn O'Connor

FACING PAGE BOTTOM LEFT: A soft arched ceiling and vanity face in bookmatched and sequenced afromosia veneer with cross-banded borders creates a cozy environment. Arched ceilings and white onyx floors and tops are consistent throughout the suite.
Photograph by Beth Singer

FACING PAGE BOTTOM RIGHT: We used a fiddleback maple, herringbone pattern to create bookmatching and symmetry over the walls, which provide an exquisite nook for a demilune-shaped vanity with veneered lumber Queen Anne legs.
Photograph by Beth Singer

"Inspiration comes from the space itself—the existing architecture dictates the style."

—Greg Bartelt

ABOVE: Antique Victorian arches with restored hand-carved elements anchor the entertainment room. The complex coffered ceiling plays off of the arches while accommodating a dropdown projector and subtly integrated pin lighting. We used all quartersawn white oak lumber construction. Interior design by Interior Corp.
Photograph by George Dzahristos

FACING PAGE: Installed in one piece, a dramatic oval stepped ceiling ring wreathes the dining area. We paneled the perimeter walls in crotch mahogany, an elegant counterpoint to the 23-carat silverleaf scalloped frieze. With inlaid polished nickel, our mahogany copy of a Ruhlmann dining table in pomele dominates the space while, in the background, a macassar ebony elliptical secondary dining table with high gloss polyester finish offers comfortable, less formal accommodations. An antique Deco light fixture pulls the room together. Interior design by Walter Herz Interiors.
Photograph by Beth Singer

"We pride ourselves in being both imaginative and hands-on. This artistic precision builds spaces full of emotion, wit, and surprise."

—Douglas Hoerr

living the elements

Douglas Hoerr was in high school when he first saw a landscape architect's drawing for turning the quarry in his Indiana hometown into a recreation area. "I was blown away by the transformative power of a plan on paper," he recalls. After earning a landscape architecture degree at Purdue, he combined his interest in design with a passion for building things during the next 10 years at a great-uncle's landscape firm in Peoria. Relishing the hands-on education, Doug left the firm for a two-year gardening sabbatical in England, where he worked in the personal gardens of three of Britain's most-respected garden designers. He credits the daily work in the gardens alongside these masters for his knowledge of plant species and his sensitivity to the art of building spaces for gracious living.

Doug returned home in 1991 to establish his Chicago design firm. Today, he and his partner Peter Schaudt lead a firm of 40 landscape architects, designers, architects, horticulturists, and LEED-accredited professionals. Though it specializes in design, the firm's keen attention to craftsmanship frequently brings designers to project sites, quarries, and nurseries to make selections and direct owners' contractors. Doug explains, "Our aim is to create destinations and experiences that delight, season after season."

Hoerr Schaudt Landscape Architects

"We are unafraid to reimagine the space and to bring it into true harmony with the terrain and the existing built environment."

—Douglas Hoerr

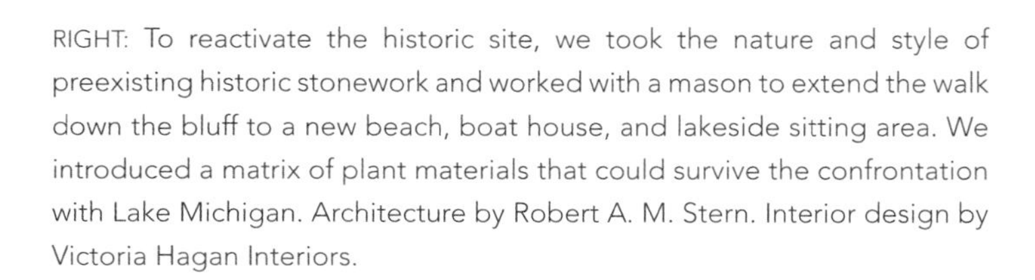

RIGHT: To reactivate the historic site, we took the nature and style of preexisting historic stonework and worked with a mason to extend the walk down the bluff to a new beach, boat house, and lakeside sitting area. We introduced a matrix of plant materials that could survive the confrontation with Lake Michigan. Architecture by Robert A. M. Stern. Interior design by Victoria Hagan Interiors.

PREVIOUS PAGES: We extended the tranquil experience of a garden surrounding a century-old house in Lake Forest, Illinois. We found mature crab trees to match several that existed on the property and wove them together into a full, shady allée. To deepen the sense of mystery and discovery, we designed a gate and hedge to reveal the entrance to a sunken water garden. A restrained response to the site, the handsome and elegant garden provides enjoyment four seasons of the year.
Photographs by Linda Oyama Bryan

"Our exterior design is an interplay of romance, classical order, natural abundance, and emotive expression, always at a human scale."

—Douglas Hoerr

ABOVE: We used undulating boxwood hedges and old-fashioned iron arches to support climbing roses that define the room's "ceiling." The homeowners and their guests dine alfresco within the curves of the serpentine promenade while tomatoes in the pots up front add honesty and delight to the garden.

FACING PAGE TOP: A special entrance invites young ones into a "children's garden." We used boxwood in a playful way with fun annual combinations and bulbs for flower cutting.

FACING PAGE BOTTOM: We carried the Italianate styling of this Lincoln Park home into its landscape elements. The dining terrace will continue to feel more secluded from its urban surroundings as vines make their way across the pergola's exposed, reclaimed timbers over time. Architecture by Carr Warner Architects. Interior design by Terese Messina Designs.

Photographs by Linda Oyama Bryan

"Sometimes subtle responses are the most powerful—our aim is to make you wonder where we left off and nature began."

—Douglas Hoerr

ABOVE: Dozens of varieties of clematis climb this oak-beam and brick pergola designed to appear plucked from the English countryside. We responded to the Tudor-style architecture of the home with complementary materials and style, but the overall design fits the needs of contemporary life. A room within the woods, the feature extends the family's living space outside and creates the bones that hold up in the winter.
Photograph by Linda Oyama Bryan

FACING PAGE: We nestled a new house into an established city neighborhood so that it doesn't seem large and imposing. Large blocks of Wisconsin stone, mature birch trees, and strong geometric patterns in the landscape match the boldness of the house. Lush ground cover and vibrant seasonal changes cushion the home and invite exploration. Architecture by Booth Hansen. Interior design by Semel Snow Interior Design.
Photograph by Doug Snower

"We think a lot about how a landscape will be experienced—where there will be invitations to pause, peruse, or view, where it is natural to create moments of structure or moments of flow."

—Douglas Hoerr

ABOVE: On an old farm in Northern Michigan, we've created a series of courtyards, carving spaces out of the natural landscape and reinforcing them with stone walls. A 110-foot saltwater lap pool leads into a camouflaged utility structure. Everything above the wall returns to wild landscape while everything below the wall emulates the language of the house. The homeowners watch the seasons change as Russian sage dominates after thousands of alium gigantium have bloomed. Architecture by Rugo Raff Architects. Interior design by Tom Stringer Design Partners.
Photograph by Henry B. Joy IV

FACING PAGE TOP: A simple, restrained approach for this summer retreat takes advantage of the common space shared with other properties and highlights the premier advantage of the home's location: the view of the lake. Architecture by von Weise Associates. Interior design by Suzanne Lovell.
Photograph by Doug Snower

FACING PAGE BOTTOM: Wall fountains spill water at different heights, creating ambient sound that muffles noise from the interstate a mile away. We worked closely with the architect to design the fountain next to the Illinois country home's screened porch. Architecture by Marvin Herman & Associates. Interior design by Semel Snow Interior Design.
Photograph by Linda Oyama Bryan

"Landscape is not a static thing. We think of it as a theatrical setting in which actions take place—the actions of nature and the actions of people."

—Douglas Hoerr

ABOVE: The perfect companion to a contemporary home, a clean stone deck extends the home's living space right up to the edge of the Lake Michigan bluff. Water pours off the lakeside edge of the infinity pool into a streamlined waterfall, audibly emphasizing the presence of water as you descend a stair to the beach below. From the deck, a streamlined cable railing preserves the view. Architecture by R. Scott Javore & Associates. Interior design by Petra Adelfang Design.
Photograph by Linda Oyama Bryan

RIGHT: We've created a cloistered, sunken courtyard in the middle of the city. The owners can relax on the dining terrace and enjoy the serenity of the water garden. Architecture by Booth Hansen. Interior design by Semel Snow Interior Design.
Photograph by Michelle Litvin

FACING PAGE TOP: Viewed from the kitchen, a Zen garden retains its sense of stillness and beauty even in the winter. The stepping stone path complements the lawn's simplicity while providing counterpoint to antique Asian urns containing echeveria and sedums. Architecture by Wheeler Kearns Architects.
Photograph by Scott Shigley

FACING PAGE BOTTOM: For a family that likes to entertain, we introduced the freestanding elements of backlit glass panels. Water cascades over the top, creating ambient sounds, while trees block the urban sprawl beyond. The black, stained-concrete table serves multiple purposes—for sitting on, using as a cocktail table, or roasting marshmallows—and the fire option extends the space's usage from early spring into late fall. Interior design by Matt Lorenz.
Photograph by Scott Shigley

Platinum Poolcare Aquatech, Ltd.

Wheeling, Illinois

"All aspects of the design project should be examined. We dive deeply into people's lifestyle needs and preferences to create a highly personalized aesthetic."

—James D. Atlas

ABOVE: Connecting the outdoors to the indoors, the dramatic resort-style pool features a rock grotto and tunnel that leads the swimmer to a walk-up sauna lined with handmade imported tiles from Wales. Cave paintings and creatively crafted stalactites hang from its ceilings for an authentic look.

FACING PAGE: As the perfect complement to an uber-contemporary glass home, we designed a simple geometric-shaped pool to fit flawlessly into the tight urban space. We created volume by utilizing several elevation changes to incorporate the raised spa, water feature, and swimming pool. *Photographs courtesy of Outvision Photography*

"Pools should fit seamlessly into the environment and emphasize the indoor-outdoor connection."

—James D. Atlas

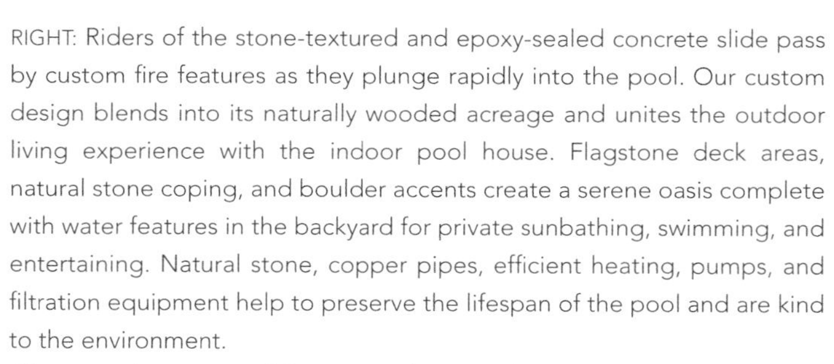

RIGHT: Riders of the stone-textured and epoxy-sealed concrete slide pass by custom fire features as they plunge rapidly into the pool. Our custom design blends into its naturally wooded acreage and unites the outdoor living experience with the indoor pool house. Flagstone deck areas, natural stone coping, and boulder accents create a serene oasis complete with water features in the backyard for private sunbathing, swimming, and entertaining. Natural stone, copper pipes, efficient heating, pumps, and filtration equipment help to preserve the lifespan of the pool and are kind to the environment.
Photograph courtesy of Outvision Photography

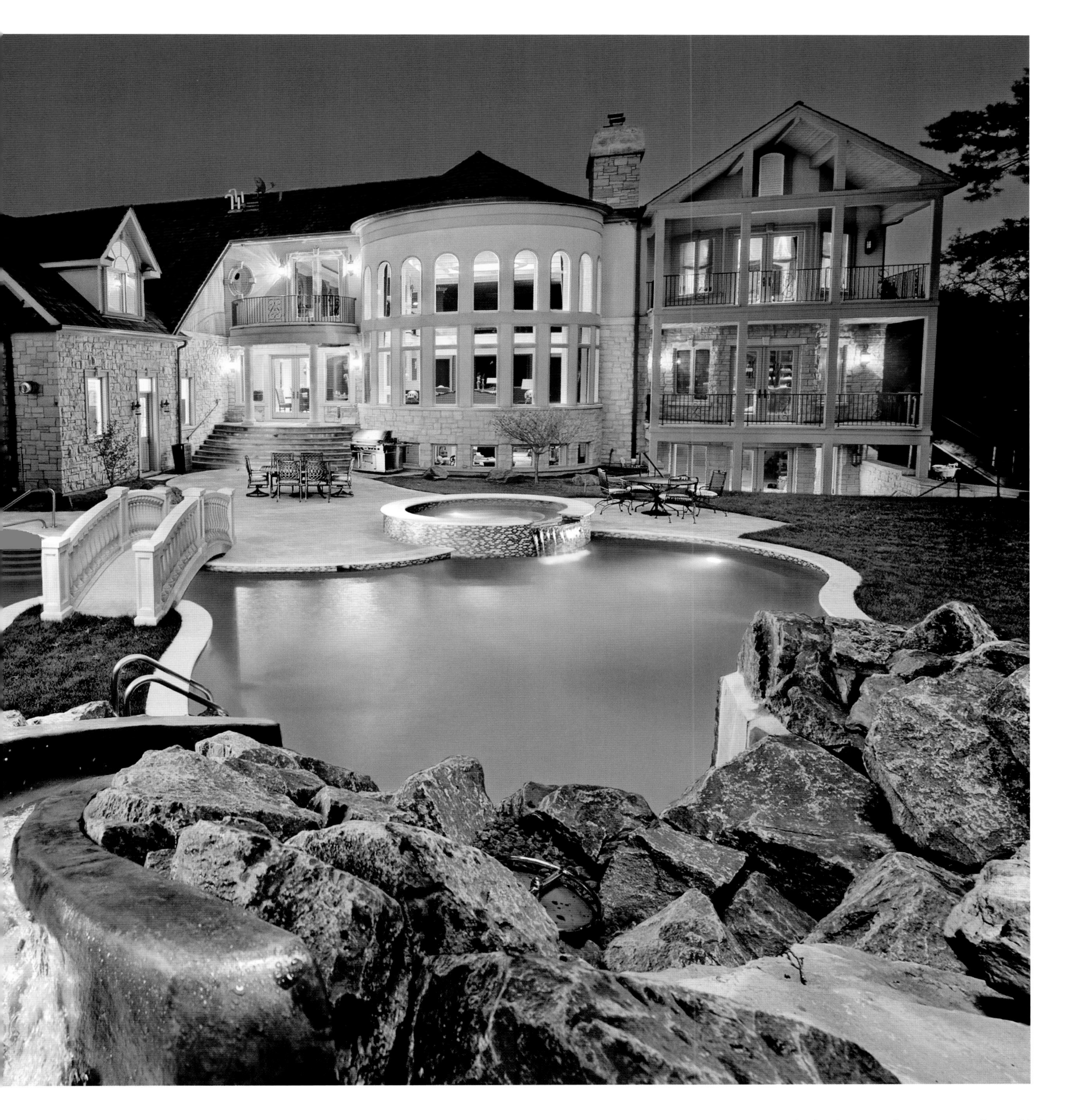

RIGHT: The elliptical-shaped indoor pool takes on an ocean blue glow when illuminated at night. Underwater lighting is an art form, and we are adept to plan, design, and create special effects that reflect the homeowner's taste. We integrated eco-friendly principles and superior technical systems to provide both form and function.

FACING PAGE: We were commissioned to create freeform outdoor pools that showcase beautiful perspectives with varying levels of several bodies of water. Behind the scenes, our designs reveal engineering innovations, security features, and hydraulics with superior structural solutions and equipment for the ultimate swimming experience. One pool's interior coating was custom blended to achieve a Caribbean turquoise color for a mesmerizing lagoon look. Ornamental gas-powered fire bowls with electronic ignitions have red glass effects to look like molten rock when burning.
Photographs courtesy of Linda Oyama Bryan

"A custom pool should be the exclamation point of a residence and a true reflection of the homeowner's sense of style."

—Terry Smith

ABOVE LEFT: The signature cantilevered seashell design is actually a swim-through entrance to the indoor pool from the connecting tunnel and cave. This theatrical element was hand sculpted and structurally made of the same fiberglass material used in fabricating the hull of a yacht. Its custom lining is an iridescent finish to resemble mother-of-pearl and the textural, faux-coral ceramic tile covers the shell's exterior for a natural effect. The eye-catching, fantasy shell uses extremely complex technology.

ABOVE RIGHT: Our overall design of the indoor pool was based on a more formal, sophisticated vision. The chiffon scarf is made of handmade tile imported from Wales, inlaid to form the blue and white nautical stripe design flowing down the pool stairs. We commissioned an artisan to make elegant, curvilinear railings of brushed stainless steel to complement the pool.

FACING PAGE: Daylight floods the natatorium to showcase the details from its one-of-a-kind seashell to the Italian travertine floors and automated windows.
Photographs courtesy of Linda Oyama Bryan

ABOVE: A Zen-inspired hydrotherapy pool suited to urban living also has an automatic cover that retracts under the coping of Pennsylvania bluestone. Both the pool and spa feature automatic pool covers with custom stone vanishing lid systems for safety and heat retention. Our efficient design allows the spa and pool to remain open in the colder fall and winter months without excessive energy bills.
Photograph courtesy of Outvision Photography

FACING PAGE TOP: We brought exotic flair and island inspiration to a sprawling suburban Northbrook home. Our 2,000-square-foot freeform swimming pool showcases native Wisconsin dolomitic limestone coping; the natural stone marries perfectly to the Turkish marble decking. A unique architectural bridge connects two sides of the pool. We had the bridge made of solid limestone for its aesthetic superiority and high quality that will surely stand the test of time.
Photograph courtesy of Outvision Photography

FACING PAGE BOTTOM: Fiber-optic lighting creates colorful illuminated effects; hidden flow jet fountains add a festive touch. We removed the home's original pool and created an impressive two-tiered rectangular swimming pool and spa with a natural Turkish travertine deck.
Photograph courtesy of Linda Oyama Bryan

Night Light, Inc., Landscape Illumination

Lombard, Illinois

"Exterior illumination should tell the landscape's story after dark by providing visual harmony between the key site and landscape elements."

—Dean MacMorris

ABOVE: Beautiful landscape illumination accentuates all of the home's charming exterior elements—most notably, the pergola, which is accented to entice people to come out and enjoy the space. The growing popularity of the "staycation" has made it increasingly more popular to bring outdoor features to life and give them prominence.

FACING PAGE: The motorcourt leads to a stately fountain that warmly glows to emphasize the rich details of the stonework while the two trees beyond are bathed in cool uplighting that highlights their lush, healthy appearance. A series of coach lights along the drive guides the way to the entrance.
Photographs by Linda Oyama Bryan

"When nighttime falls, we use light as a paintbrush to enhance the beauty of the landscape while providing safety and security."

—Dean MacMorris

ABOVE: Moonlight and cool uplighting cast a crisp glow on landscape elements, creating a sense of space, while warm lighting suffuses the pergola. The melding of different tones and qualities of light unifies the landscape and affords a seamless transition between spaces.

FACING PAGE TOP & BOTTOM LEFT: The beautiful architecture is featured as part of the exterior composition by bringing out some of the key stone features and architectural elements. The home and landscape work in harmony to create a soft ambience of understated elegance.

FACING PAGE BOTTOM RIGHT: Connecting upper and lower spaces, the stone path has an informal, natural look. We echoed that feeling by downplaying the presence of lighting fixtures and specifying just enough light to make the walkway safe and beautiful.

Photographs by Linda Oyama Bryan

"The dark is as important as the light."

—Mitchell Beiser

ABOVE: Working with the bronze fountain and existing entryway lights, we created drama by highlighting key architectural features, stonework details, and landscape elements; certain areas intentionally fall into shadow to create depth. A minimal quantity of carefully placed lighting fixtures produces the most natural and pleasing results.
Photograph by Norb Hansen

FACING PAGE TOP: A long serpentine driveway lined with staggered lampposts leads to the home, which is set on significant acreage. With cool lights on the landscape and warm lights on the architecture, the home stands as the clear focal point. When we're designing in a rural setting with limited ambient light, it's even more important than usual to illuminate selectively. Mystery and drama result when shadows are used to punctuate the highlights.
Photograph by Linda Oyama Bryan

FACING PAGE BOTTOM: Taking cues from the natural fieldstone façade, hand-hewn beams, wrought-iron details, and stone patio, we created a very natural lighting scheme. The moonlit feeling comes from mercury vapor fixtures that are well-concealed in the trees. The space is lit well enough to keep guests from tripping but not so brightly that the warmth of candles is lost, creating a distinct outdoor experience.
Photographs by Norb Hansen

Prairie Restorations

Princeton, Minnesota

"We do for the earth what doctors do for the sick. Our patient is the land; restoring and maintaining the health of local plant communities is our top priority."

—Ron Bowen

ABOVE: Set in the Minneapolis suburb of Plymouth, a home landscape captures the allure of the Minnesota prairie in July. We created a garden—a concept that includes selected elements and careful design to accurately represent the natural prairie.
Photograph by Mike Evenocheck

FACING PAGE: With the nation's growing awareness of ecological concerns, companies have been moving toward presenting a strong image of compassion. When we worked with the leadership of the Lake Region Electric Cooperative in central Minnesota, they wanted to show their care and concern for indigenous preservation.
Photograph by Ron Bowen

"Sincerity lies at the heart of the company. We started with genuine compassion, a logical idea, and the sturdiness of my old pick-up truck. And the sentiment has caught on—society notices the importance of what we've been doing for more than 30 years."

—Ron Bowen

ABOVE LEFT: The prairie is a delicate ecosystem, storing soil and carbon to nurture flora and fauna. A midsummer scene demonstrates this as a Monarch butterfly sits amongst butterfly milkweed, pink phlox, and black-eyed Susans.

ABOVE RIGHT: We gave charm to an open, rural residential site with careful orientation of each plant. Butterfly milkweed, vervain, and yellow coreopsis grow to the edge of the landowner's home.

FACING PAGE: My background has given me the tools to focus on the biological aspect of our work. Studies in forestry and a master's degree in landscape architecture have given me a technical base to work from and allow me to share the appeal of the land, in both function and form. A tallgrass prairie was restored for conservation and aesthetic purposes. The open countryside shows off prairie phlox and a variety of grasses in June.
Photographs by Ron Bowen

perspectives ON DESIGN

GREAT LAKES TEAM

ASSOCIATE PUBLISHER: Heidi Nessa
GRAPHIC DESIGNER: Paul Strength
EDITOR: Michael C. McConnell
PRODUCTION COORDINATOR: Drea Williams

HEADQUARTERS TEAM

PUBLISHER: Brian G. Carabet
PUBLISHER: John A. Shand
EXECUTIVE PUBLISHER: Phil Reavis
PUBLICATION & CIRCULATION MANAGER: Lauren B. Castelli
SENIOR GRAPHIC DESIGNER: Emily A. Kattan
GRAPHIC DESIGNER: Kendall Muellner
MANAGING EDITOR: Rosalie Z. Wilson
EDITOR: Anita M. Kasmar
EDITOR: Jennifer Nelson
EDITOR: Sarah Tangney
EDITOR: Lindsey Wilson
MANAGING PRODUCTION COORDINATOR: Kristy Randall
PROJECT COORDINATOR: Laura Greenwood
TRAFFIC COORDINATOR: Brandi Breaux
ADMINISTRATIVE MANAGER: Carol Kendall
CLIENT SUPPORT COORDINATOR: Amanda Mathers

PANACHE PARTNERS, LLC
CORPORATE HEADQUARTERS
1424 Gables Court
Plano, TX 75075
469.246.6060
www.panache.com
www.panachedesign.com

Hoerr Schaudt Landscape Architects, page 205

index

Platinum Poolcare Aquatech, Ltd., page 217

THE PANACHE COLLECTION

CREATING SPECTACULAR PUBLICATIONS FOR DISCERNING READERS

Dream Homes Series

An Exclusive Showcase of the Finest Architects, Designers and Builders

Carolinas
Chicago
Coastal California
Colorado
Deserts
Florida
Georgia
Los Angeles
Metro New York
Michigan
Minnesota
New England
New Jersey
Northern California
Ohio & Pennsylvania
Pacific Northwest
Philadelphia
South Florida
Southwest
Tennessee
Texas
Washington, D.C.

Perspectives on Design Series

Design Philosophies Expressed by Leading Professionals

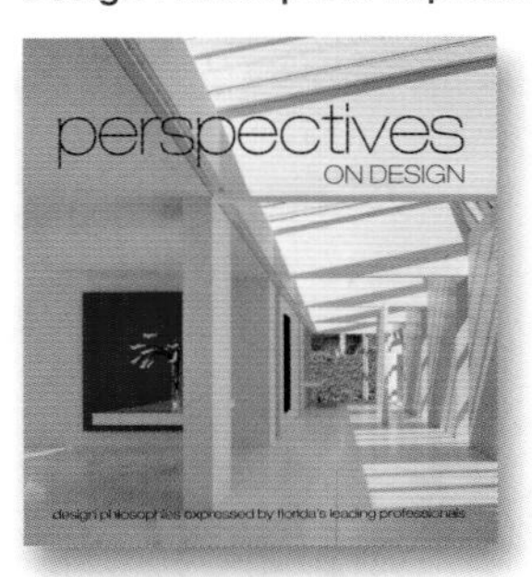

California
Carolinas
Chicago
Colorado
Florida
Georgia
Great Lakes
Minnesota
New England
New York
Pacific Northwest
Southwest
Western Canada

Spectacular Wineries Series

A Captivating Tour of Established, Estate and Boutique Wineries

California's Central Coast
Napa Valley
New York
Sonoma County

City by Design Series

An Architectural Perspective

Atlanta
Charlotte
Chicago
Dallas
Denver
Orlando
Phoenix
San Francisco
Texas

Spectacular Homes Series

An Exclusive Showcase of the Finest Interior Designers

California
Carolinas
Chicago
Colorado
Florida
Georgia
Heartland
London
Michigan
Minnesota
New England
Metro New York
Ohio & Pennsylvania
Pacific Northwest
Philadelphia
South Florida
Southwest
Tennessee
Texas
Toronto
Washington, D.C.
Western Canada

Art of Celebration Series

The Making of a Gala

Chicago & the Greater Midwest
Georgia
New England
New York
Philadelphia
South Florida
Southern California
Southwest
Texas
Toronto
Washington, D.C.
Wine Country

Specialty Titles

The Finest in Unique Luxury Lifestyle Publications

Cloth and Culture: Couture Creations of Ruth E. Funk
Distinguished Inns of North America
Extraordinary Homes California
Geoffrey Bradfield Ex Arte
Into the Earth: A Wine Cave Renaissance
Spectacular Golf of Colorado
Spectacular Golf of Texas
Spectacular Hotels
Spectacular Restaurants of Texas
Visions of Design

PanacheDesign.com

Where the Design Industry's Finest Professionals Gather, Share, and Inspire

PanacheDesign.com overflows with innovative ideas from leading architects, builders, interior designers, and other specialists. A gallery of design photographs and library of advice-oriented articles are among the comprehensive site's offerings.

Panache Partners, LLC   1424 Gables Court   Plano, Texas 75075   469.246.6060   www.panache.com